An Open Book and Empty Cup

London Regained

IQBAL AHMED

To
Vanora,
Warm wishes!
Iqbal Ahmed

COLDSTREAM PUBLISHERS
C

First Published in Great Britain in 2020 by
COLDSTREAM PUBLISHERS
9 Juliana Close,
London N2 0TJ
coldstream.publishers@hotmail.com

Designed and produced in Great Britain by
Clinton Smith Design

A CIP catalogue record for this book is available from the British Library.

ISBN 978-1-5272-5321-6

This book is dedicated to all of those,

past and present,

who have found themselves

lost in London.

FOREWORD

The latest book by Iqbal Ahmed, who was born and raised in Kashmir, is in large part a love letter to London, where he has lived and worked for the last twenty-five years.

In his previous critically acclaimed books, Iqbal focused on the hopes and predicaments of fellow-immigrants in London, the British Isles and Germany. In this, his fourth book, he reflects on London itself and his changing personal reactions to it over the years as a dedicated cyclist, coffee house habitué, hotel worker and father of an inquisitive young boy. The book also offers poignant insights into Iqbal's country of origin.

His perspective as an immigrant enables him to make unusual comparisons and to see London from unfamiliar angles: things that native Londoners might take for granted, he finds interesting, intriguing, and even extraordinary. The book includes chapters on such themes as the vagaries of borders, cycling in London at night, the allure of hotels, and the hazards of travel in Kashmir today; and there is a searching look at a single affluent street, The Bishops Avenue in Hampstead.

Iqbal takes the reader on many an interesting detour – the mark of a true *flâneur* – as his observations weave back and forth in time and location, his impressions of London evoking potent memories of his early years in Srinagar as well as his later visits there. Seeing London through the eyes of this quietly subtle and probing writer in turn enables the reader to discover the city afresh.

Neil Hornick
London, November 2019

AUTHOR'S NOTE

When I set out to write *An Open Book and Empty Cup*, Jammu and Kashmir was a semi-autonomous state. Before the end of my journey, it was relegated to a Union Territory, but I have let it remain a state in my book. Since the region remains volatile and since Great Britain itself is going through a period of unpredictable change, I apologise for any other discrepancies that may have arisen since the book went to press. However, some lapses are no doubt attributable to flawed memory, which sometimes works in mysterious ways.

My fiftieth year had come and gone,
I sat, a solitary man,
In a crowded London shop,
An open book and empty cup
On the marble table-top.

Vacillation

W. B. Yeats, 1865-1939

Contents

Bordering on the Absurd

When the first result of the Brexit referendum came in from Gibraltar on that fateful night in June 2016, it gave me false hope that other results would follow suit and Britain would remain in the EU. The people of Gibraltar had overwhelmingly voted to remain. It wasn't surprising, though, because they know all too well what it means to be isolated, having a closed border with Spain from 1969 to 1982.

I awoke next morning to discover that the Leavers had won the referendum by a narrow margin. Derek Walcott's verse from *Omeros* reverberated in my perplexed mind:

> And now I would wake up, troubled and inexact
> from that shallow sleep in which dreams precede sunrise,
> as the vague mind cautiously acknowledges the fact

Later that day, I met an Irish guest at the hotel where I work and expressed my dismay at the result of the referendum. He burst out laughing and said that he was telling all his British friends that the UK is very welcome to become Ireland's fifth province. But it wasn't long before his mood darkened. He told me that he often drove from Southern to Northern Ireland for work and it would be a nightmare to go through a border control again.

The UK's borders are delineated by its coastline. I still find it bizarre to see signs stating 'UK BORDER' when I arrive at Heathrow airport, which is 100 miles inland from the legendary White Cliffs of Dover. Once established as a long-term London resident, I yearned for the day when I could roam throughout Europe without need of a visa.

The word 'border' has got dire associations in my native Kashmir. The broken line on the map that divides Kashmir into three parts is called a Line of Control (LoC) on the western side and Line of Actual Control (LAC) on the eastern side. I realized it was military jargon only after an English acquaintance in London asked me what the Line of Control is. I explained that if you should drift from one side to another while rambling near the border in Kashmir, your life will be at risk in trying to return to your side.

There is no defined border where the two sides of the broken line meet in the middle of the map of Kashmir. But it is the location of one of the longest mountain glaciers in the world and hence a fragile environment. Both the Indian and Pakistani armies have placed heavy artillery in the snow there to ward each other off. It is certainly the most preposterous border confrontation anywhere in the world and has earned the glacier the dubious accolade of being the highest battleground on the planet.

As a child, I preferred to browse those pages of my Bartholomew Atlas, bought at the Kashmir Bookshop in Srinagar, that depicted the physical rather than political terrain. The physical maps had the contours of mountain peaks drawn on them and showed snow-fed rivers flowing freely from one side to another without any regard for a *de facto* border. However, it wasn't until quite recently, when I travelled to Zanskar, that I saw with my own eyes the River Suru flowing gently through a valley. It crosses the Line of Control downriver and joins the Indus on the other side.

The state of Jammu and Kashmir is roughly the same size as the UK and the dispute over its borders began in the aftermath of the Raj. The Empire is long gone and Britain is left with only 14 overseas territories – a shadow of her former self. Gibraltar is one of those territories. As a result of Brexit, a semantic row has broken out between Britain and the EU as to whether an erstwhile crown colony can properly be described as a colony any more.

Before travelling to Gibraltar, I was warned by a Spanish friend about a town at its border called La Linea that was reputed to be a gateway for narcotics. It's much cheaper to buy cigarettes in Gibraltar than Spain, he said. Cigarette smuggling has evolved into a full-scale drugs trade in La Linea and now 5% of its population is involved in this illicit business. But that is hardly surprising given that one third of the town's residents are unemployed. He told me that I should instead visit Marinaleda in Seville, where the cost of living is low and the rate of employment very high.

Eventually, in 2010, I was overjoyed to be able to visit a European country from the UK without requiring a visa. It felt as if I belonged to a vast continent rather than a small country; and I considered it to be a privilege to live in a land that was a member of the EU. Never could I have imagined that it might all come to an end before the decade was over.

The word 'border' evokes nationalistic feelings on both sides of the Atlantic these days. The plan to build a wall across the Mexico-US border sits well with the convictions of those people in Britain who want to leave the EU. And as in medieval times, when a moat around the Tower of London kept danger at bay, Britain is in retreat from the EU.

I had found the freedom of movement within the EU very exhilarating and marvelled at the ease with which one could cross a border from one country into another. It was a very long way, in every sense, from the border skirmishes in my beloved Kashmir.

The biggest threat of our times comes from climate change, which recognises no borders. America has already withdrawn from the Paris Agreement, and Britain may leave the EU Emissions Trading Scheme after Brexit. Likewise, cybercrime has no regard for national borders and poses a threat to individuals and institutions in every country. Border screening is not even effective in stopping a pandemic. The reality is that we are living in a world of multi-layered interdependence.

My Spanish friend asked me why I wanted to travel to Gibraltar. After all, he said, it's only a rock. I told him that I'd heard that you could enter Hades, the Greek underworld, from one of the caves in the rock and I would like to go there to drink from Lethe, the river of oblivion, so I could forget the lamentable outcome of the Brexit referendum.

I asked an English friend a few days before the referendum whether he had changed his mind about voting for Britain to leave the EU. He said in a matter-of-fact way that it was bad enough for him to tolerate me, let alone all those people who have arrived in Britain recently and were receiving state benefits, and he emphasized that Britain was only a small island.

I was invited for a meal at the home of a friend from Kashmir when I arrived in the UK 25 years ago. He was married to an Englishwoman. When the dinner table conversation digressed to the subject of Imperialism, my friend's wife said that Britain was herself colonised by the Romans twenty centuries ago. It was bizarre for me to hear such a historical fact since I had grown up in Kashmir only knowing Britain as an Imperial power that played the Great Game in our part of the world with another Imperial power – Russia. It therefore seemed preposterous to me to hear campaigners for Britain to leave the EU insisting that they wanted the UK's independence from the EU. I could only associate the word 'independence' with the British Raj.

When I arrived in London in June 1994, there was no

rail link between the UK and continental Europe. The first direct train from Paris arrived at Waterloo a few months later to much fanfare. I went to the station to meet a friend visiting the UK. He was from Kashmir but had lived in Colorado for many years and was an American passport holder. When I met him at the station he seemed a bit flustered and told me that an immigration officer at Waterloo station had stopped and questioned him but let in his fellow Americans standing in the queue before him without asking any questions. He felt that perhaps it was because of his dark complexion.

I marvelled at the idea of taking a train from the centre of London to Paris Gare du Nord. However, I neither had the means nor a visa to make a trip to France. But many years later I joined a long queue outside the French Embassy in Kensington to apply for a visa. When I finally got in after a lengthy wait outside I saw a poster for the Womack & Womack duo that featured the loaded word 'Respect'. It made me smile because of its use as a formal greeting and because I had met this husband-and-wife team as guests at the hotel where I worked and found them very amiable. The Eurostar didn't depart from Waterloo station any more and I had to go to St Pancras to catch my train. As it entered the tunnel under the English Channel it became dark and blurry. When it emerged on the other side of the tunnel, I noticed that the design of the pylons in the green fields had changed from the one I was accustomed to seeing in Britain and India, and it felt good to visit Paris after a gap of two decades.

I had spent many evenings in the West End during my first few years in London and got to know the streets around there pretty well. One day I was walking down the Strand when I overheard someone mention the name of a theatre. I stopped and saw two women, apparently a mother and daughter, who looked lost but seemed reluctant to ask anyone for directions. I pointed them in the right direction for the theatre. The teenage girl asked me in a direct and honest way how I knew the location and they didn't, while her mother looked simply perplexed. I thought that perhaps they had come to London from the countryside and didn't expect much civility in the town.

At the Edinburgh Festival a few years ago I happened to mention how insular England could be if you are an outsider. Someone in the audience asked me if I had been to the countryside. Well, the countryside has spoken in the recent referendum and now I have no wish to live there. I consider myself lucky to be living in London where a majority have voted to remain in the EU. The rise of populism in the UK is threatening its liberal values. Our European neighbours feel that Britons are nostalgic about the days of the Raj and may very likely revert to Imperial weights and measures once the country has exited the EU.

The majority of people living in the UK have turned their backs on the biggest peace project in the world by voting to leave the Union. However, Britain has still got a linguistic hold on the EU. It has 24 official languages but it is English that is usually spoken at its press conferences, and when a UK MEP or the head of Her Majesty's Government takes to the floor, they usually appear to be larger than life figures just by virtue of speaking their own language. The heads of European institutions speak the language of the British people who, for their part, do not reciprocate.

I found it amusing when an English lawyer I once visited with a friend who is also a lawyer referred to him disdainfully as a foreigner. I occasionally hear from my English acquaintances that this country isn't what it used to be before people from Eastern Europe moved to London to find work. A Polish friend who has lived in London for over 10 years told me some time ago that it was a dog's life to have to depend on two low-paid jobs just to survive in the UK; he hurried from one place of work to another during the course of the day and he sometimes crossed paths with elderly English folk walking their dogs in a park, aware that many of these people had voted for Britain to leave the EU.

The 23rd of June was indeed a sad day for Europe. Those who have rocked the boat seem to be calm and composed. But those Britons who wanted to uphold liberal values will lament this day for many years to come.

*

The town of Uri in Kashmir belongs to folklore. Although it is less than 70 miles away from Srinagar it is best known for being a remote outpost. When I was a child, my mother recounted stories about her eldest and favourite uncle who was stationed there as a civil servant. She was fond of mentioning an old power station at Mohra and how close it was to the actual Line of Control in Uri. Mohra became a mythical place in my imagination. I have travelled just once to Baramulla, which is halfway between Srinagar and Uri.

The River Jhelum wanders through Srinagar to feed Lake Wular and then drops into a gorge passing through the Pir Panjal mountains before reaching Uri. The power station at Mohra is more than a century old. A new hydro-electric power station was built in this garrison town in the 1990s by a Swedish company, Skanska, which was part of the consortium called Uri Civil. Foreign tourists had already stopped visiting Srinagar by the end of the 1980s and some of the houseboat owners in Lake Dal rented their taxis to the construction company that was building the power station at Uri. Then one day two of the Swedish engineers working in Kashmir were kidnapped and the project ran into difficulties.

Muzaffarabad is located downriver on the other side of the Line of Control. The River Jhelum flows into Mangla Dam near Mirpur and then crosses into Punjab where there is a town of the same name located on its right bank. The river is believed to be the Bidaspes, mentioned by Ptolemy. It joins the Chenab river in Jhang.

Convoys of army trucks are a common sight if you are travelling through Kashmir. As a child I used to count the number of trucks in a convoy that overtook the car or bus I was travelling in. It's an unwritten rule of the highway code in Kashmir that military vehicles have the right of way, so when troops travel from one cantonment to another, motorists will usually give way to them on narrow roads. However, my father made a mistake a few months after he passed his driving test. He was driving an Ambassador car on a hilly road from Srinagar to Jammu and failed to give way to a military man. The driver behind him put his foot down until my father realised that the gap between his car and the truck had vanished. Thus he was taught a valuable lesson. Many years later, I had a somewhat similar experience while travelling in a taxi from Kargil to Srinagar with some friends. The taxi driver was in his early twenties and reluctant to let an army vehicle overtake him on a winding road. He was soon ordered to pull over by an army officer at a place where a lot of army trucks were parked near a campsite. We were ordered out of the taxi, questioned by the officer and asked to show our IDs. One of my friends was so outraged that I had to pacify him or we would have never made it to Srinagar.

I visited Kashmir in the summer of 2012 when some of the bunkers used by security forces in the town had been removed and domestic tourists were flocking to Srinagar again. I rode in a car travelling a few miles out of Srinagar and saw a long line of paramilitary men patrolling a country road adjoining a paddy field. They carried automatic rifles and seemed to be on edge. The person who drove me that day told me that it was a daily exercise for these men to walk from one camp to another. I also remember waiting for a bus with my mother on a desolate road at the outskirts of the town when I was eight or nine years old and a convoy of military trucks appeared. My mother held my hand firmly and I realised she was trembling with fear until the convoy had gone out of sight.

It is hard to imagine that the Line of Control in Kashmir is just a few miles away from the tourist resort of Gulmarg. The cable car project there had taken forever to finish and I had never taken a ride on a Gondola (as it is locally known) until a few years ago when I visited the mountain resort for a night. The second stage of the cable car ascent terminates before reaching the top of the mountain. I wanted to scale the peak but my friends advised me against it, explaining that it was off-limits for civilians. Hoping it wasn't true, I walked a short distance towards the top but when I saw a soldier with a gun slung across his back I immediately returned to the cable car station and spotted an army camp situated not far from it. People who ski from the top of this mountain in winter are usually afraid of losing their way and ending up in an army camp.

On my visit to Srinagar in August 2016, I got up very early in the morning to catch a return flight to Delhi in the afternoon. This was because there was a curfew in the town and my parents wanted me to leave home at the break of dawn so that I didn't miss the connecting flight from Delhi. My father drove me to the airport, taking backroads until we reached a crossing closed off by concertina wire. Although we had a permit to pass through the area under curfew we weren't sure if it would be honoured by the men guarding the barricade, who belonged to the Central Reserve Police Force, as the pass was issued by a local administrator. The policeman glanced cursorily at the permit and let us through. We were stopped at a few places before reaching a road leading to the airport. The penultimate barricade was manned by local police officers. When they also started questioning my father he was unable to carry on pleading and demanded to know what the people of Kashmir had done to deserve such treatment.

The airport was busy with people who were lucky to be leaving Srinagar. As the aircraft flew over the army barracks along the runway, I caught sight of two fighter jets of the Indian Air Force parked in the concealed bays. I felt bereft by the constant bloodshed in Kashmir and a line from Walt Whitman's *Leaves of Grass* sprang to mind: 'Peace is always beautiful.' The line still rings true.

*

The word 'border', medieval in origin, derives from an Old French word, *bordeure*, which means 'the edge of a shield'. It entered the English lexicon like that other distressful word 'refugee', which also originated on the other side of the English Channel. These two words have subsequently been borrowed from the English language by scores of other languages spoken by the subjects of the British Raj. The British officers engaged in warfare in Asia for two centuries with their rival European colonisers – the French and the Dutch – in order to expand the borders of the realm of the British Monarch.

When travelling by road with a friend in 2001 from London to Edinburgh, we stopped at a viewing-point that marks an old border between England and Scotland. We found a few other motorists there, taking pictures beside a large monolith, which has the word 'England' engraved on one side and 'Scotland' on the other. It was a nice spot to enjoy a picturesque landscape but I couldn't think of it as a borderland. In fact, I thought the name 'Scottish Borders' misleading for such peaceful undulating terrain.

It is the River Tweed that forms the border between England and Scotland. I had heard the word 'tweed' since I was a small child. However, it wasn't a river that is associated with the name but a woollen fabric. The type of coarse cloth known as tweed is woven in the mills of Amritsar in Punjab and sold in Kashmir to make winter gear. My father was a cloth wholesaler. Every summer he ordered big bales of tweed from Amritsar and sold it to retailers in Srinagar before the advent of winter. But it was in London that I learnt that 'tweedy' is a derogatory term denoting someone of the rural gentry, whereas in Kashmir tweed is worn by everyone from townies to country-folk.

The textile agents from Amritsar who roamed the bazaars in Srinagar wore safari suits in summer and carried swatches of tweed in their briefcases, which by some strange coincidence always had airline tags tied to their handles. The agents took orders from wholesalers for the supply of this woollen cloth. Sometimes, as a child, I sat in my father's shop and listened intently to the conversations of these travelling businessmen, impressed by their turns of phrase and skilful sales talk. I found names like 'herringbone' and 'houndstooth' for the patterns of tweed very funny.

A type of tweed made by the recycling of old clothes is called 'shoddy'. I was astonished that the mill owners of Punjab could describe their own product in such terms. It was made by combing and spinning yarn from discarded second-hand garments. There were pedlars from Punjab who wore colourful turbans and went from door to door in Kashmir carrying huge bundles of cloth on their bicycle racks. Some of the women in Srinagar would part-exchange their old clothes for a piece of new cloth. At home in Kashmir, I could hear in the distance the street cries of these pedlars. They were particularly interested in buying women's clothes embellished with a gold-coated thread known as Zari. Some of the pedlars carried a big bundle of merchandise tied in a white cotton sheet over one shoulder and gripped horizontally before them a metal yardstick, which might double as a baton.

I once met a group of Kashmiri men in London who had travelled to Edinburgh to seek support in Scotland for Kashmiri independence. They were surprised when their hosts told them that they were also seeking their own country's independence from the UK. *À propos* of that, a Scottish friend in London once told me that he found the line 'rebellious Scots to crush' in the UK's national anthem very disconcerting.

When I flew out of Delhi's Indira Gandhi International

airport for the first time, I was more anxious whether the immigration officer at the airport would allow me to depart than whether his counterpart at Frankfurt airport would allow me into his country. Labourers who worked in the Middle East had 'Emigration Check Required' stamped on their passports and were questioned by immigration officers. These poor men were trembling in front of the officers who were like gatekeepers to another world. It was only after travelling from one European country to another that I realised that you don't necessarily have to go through immigration controls twice (the country you are travelling from and the one you are travelling to). So I found it bizarre when I took the Eurostar train from London to Paris for the first time and discovered that you can walk freely out of the Gare du Nord when the train reaches its destination.

During my first few years in London, I often went into Central London to meet a friend from Kashmir who ran a business near Chinatown and whose office was something of a meeting place for many newcomers to London. My friend liked to describe someone holding a burgundy-coloured British passport as a Red. It transported me back to the days of the Raj, when the East India Company men wore red coats, explaining why the colour red was thought of as privileged in India. I occasionally saw an Australian woman of Asian descent in my friend's office and one day she declared that she was seeking a British man for a boyfriend. Her frank admission must have broken the hearts of all the men who had gathered there, since she was an attractive woman and I thought it naïve of her to confide her longing to a bunch of men without women.

For over 20 years, I never heard British people talking about passports. However, after the Brexit referendum in 2016, when I overheard conversations in places like barbershops and the London Underground about getting a second passport from an EU country, it seemed to me like a massive reversal of fortune.

The dreaded paramilitary troops that I saw during my childhood in Kashmir belonged to the Border Security Force known only by their acronym, BSF. Whenever there was trouble in Srinagar and our local police force was unable to deal with it, the authorities in New Delhi immediately dispatched battalions of the BSF to quell the rebellion.

They wore metal helmets, padded leg guards in Khaki instead of the white ones worn by cricket players, and they carried oversized riot shields made of metal or bamboo. I was as scared by their thick moustaches as I was by their combat gear.

On my way home from school, I would sometimes come across paramilitary men sitting in a park on their protective gear, which was laid out on the ground, playing cards to while away the time. It was a menacing sight for me. The deceptive calm would suddenly be disturbed by a nearby protest and the sedentary soldiers would jump up, don their helmets and attack and scatter the crowd with long batons, aided by armed soldiers also carrying automatic weapons.

I was once walking near a park when one of these protests occurred. A European tourist who had come to see a grand mosque in Srinagar happened to be in the vicinity and asked me why everyone was running. When I told him that the BSF men would beat up anyone they could catch he wanted to know who the BSF men were. I was surprised that he'd not heard of one of the largest border security forces in the world.

The frequent skirmishes between ordinary people and paramilitary troops in Kashmir are reminiscent of scenes during the Troubles in Northern Ireland when the British army patrolled the border, swung guns and chased the mobs away with armoured vehicles made of thick metal plating with very small windows. These vehicles are nicknamed 'mousetraps' in Kashmir since they look similar to a box-like contraption that's used to catch mice. As a youngster, it was quite scary to see the paramilitaries who rode in those vehicles in Srinagar, armed with automatic weapons and their hair tied with black bandanas.

Two years after I arrived in the UK, Manchester city centre was shattered by a bomb planted by the IRA. The next day, I received a phone call from a concerned relative in Srinagar who didn't know how far Manchester was from London. It gave me much joy when the Good Friday peace agreement was signed in 1998 to end the hostilities in Ireland. It also gave me a sliver of hope that perhaps one day there would be peace in Kashmir. So many years had passed between

Bloody Sunday and the Good Friday Agreement to end the bloodshed in Ireland. It's therefore horrifying to see the foundation of a peace agreement being shaken by Brexit plus the resurrected idea of a fence at the border between Northern and Southern Ireland.

*

Some of the detractors of Irish poets living in London and other cities declared that they were untroubled by the Troubles, a claim that I consider to be mendacious. Having lived away from my native Kashmir for a long time, I can easily identify with the Irish experience. Exile can never be self-imposed; but you leave your place of birth when life there becomes so circumscribed that it is unbearable. 20th Century Irish poetry from WB Yeats to Seamus Heaney bears witness to that. When I read the poem *Vacillation* by Yeats, it was a revelation to me and I felt that this long-dead poet spoke to me directly.

I have spent much time in London coffee shops with an open book. But now that I have reached my 50th year, *Vacillation* resonates with me even more strongly. In the last year of the millennium I often sat in a coffee shop in Hampstead reading an absorbing book, with an empty cup on a table-top; and a few years later I spent many afternoons in a crowded coffee shop in Camden Town writing my own first book. However, a lot of time has slipped through my fingers since then and it is a great effort to regain lost time or the vision of an ideal place.

Cycling Home

'Habit is, of all the plants of human growth,' says Proust, 'the one that has the least need of nutritious soil in order to live, and is the first to appear on the most seemingly barren rock.' A lot of things about London life have rubbed off on me in the last 25 years. Indeed, the town itself has become a kind of bad habit. When I moved to London in 1994, I rode buses and the Underground for a couple of years until my landlady in Hampstead – a kind-hearted Punjabi woman – offered me her son's old bike for £20 and turned me into a cyclist for life.

Now I could roam the town completely at will, it felt as if I'd been granted the Freedom of the City by a worshipful livery company. I usually took bus number 24 from Hampstead to Camden Town to buy groceries at the Safeway supermarket and found it quite a drag to carry the shopping bags and wait at an inhospitable bus stop near Chalk Farm. It was then that I discovered the veracity of the adage that you can wait ages for a bus and then three come along at once. The buses in those days rarely stopped halfway to even out the service, so it was preferable to use my bike. I soon learnt how to balance shopping bags on the handlebars and glide home. The West

End of London became my backyard as I cycled there two or three times a week.

While visiting Kashmir, when someone asks me what I like about living in a big metropolis like London, I say, without giving it a second thought, that it's the cycling I like the most. But many people find my answer perplexing. One of my friends in Srinagar thought that I was pulling his leg when I met him after a long time and told him that I don't own a car in London and rely on a bike instead. He would have laughed out loud if I'd told him that it's a curse to use a car in London. Once, in a hotel in Lagos, when I asked a friendly member of staff if I could hire a pushbike, he described me as an Oyinbo – someone of European descent. He said that he would rather call an Okada – a motorcycle taxi – if I wanted to get somewhere quickly. Incidentally, someone was ingenious enough to borrow the name Okada for this service from an airline.

London used to be far behind other capital cities in Europe in the provision of bicycles, until 2010 when Transport for London introduced bikes for hire for commuters. I had found it useful to hire a similar unwieldy bike in Paris when I visited the city in 2009 and, against the advice of my friends, cycled around the Arc de Triomphe.

A few years after riding my first bike in London, I decided to buy a new one equipped with a suspension fork. The road felt a lot smoother to ride along after that. I locked my new bike to an iron fence that surrounded the front lawn of the house in which I rented a room. When I woke up in the morning, the bike had disappeared. For a few moments, I was confused and tried to remember if I had actually locked my bike to the fence the night before – until I realised that the iron fence had been cut with a hacksaw. I felt at such a loss without a bike that I went to a local shop the next day to buy another one. Unthinkingly, though, I chose a scarlet bike. Having ridden it to work, I locked it to the bike rack in the basement as usual. And when I finished work at midnight, I found that my bike had vanished. The thief must have been tempted by its brilliant red colour. However, as a courtesy, he had left a ladies bike for me in its place.

Having lost two bikes in as many days, I decided that it wasn't a good idea to buy a third one and therefore used my old bike for a few months. A few weeks later, I received an unexpected letter from the Metropolitan police, apologising that I had been the victim of a crime and stating that they couldn't find my bike. However, it didn't dissuade me from getting a new one when the old one became a real boneshaker.

For me, cycling in London is more of a necessity than a means of exercise. The price of a monthly Travelcard for Zones 1-6 in London is currently £246. This is roughly one quarter of the monthly wage of many Londoners. I was able to live within the periphery of the North Circular Road only because it hadn't cost me a penny to commute to work and back.

In 2012, when I thought I was finally quit of the spell London had cast on me and resolved to move back to Kashmir,

I was contacted by an experimental filmmaker, Marc Isaacs. He asked me to meet him in Marble Arch for the filming of the last scene of a documentary he was making about a Roman road in London that ends in Holyhead. He concluded his documentary with the sanguine words that I might put down roots in London. Marc proved to be a soothsayer. After a gap of eleven years I gradually began to regain the time that had been lost and started work on a new book. A year after Marc's prediction, my son was born.

I'd been toying for quite a long time with the idea of riding my bike a 100 miles a day, when, in September 2014, there was a cataclysmic flood in Kashmir and I felt the need to do my bit to raise some money for the victims. I quickly registered for a ride from London to Bath that was to take place in the first week of October and I had two and a half weeks to get ready for it. Since I cycle every day I didn't see the need to prepare for this ride for longer than two weeks. I still needed some training, though, before undertaking the journey.

One of my colleagues at work had recently returned from France after completing a long bike ride so I thought it would be best to seek his advice. He told me that I should train three or four times a week for the next two weeks to build my stamina and also buy the right gear for it. I resisted the idea of wearing Lycra shorts but he said it was essential to buy them if I wanted to break the 100-mile barrier in a day without getting saddle sore.

My hybrid bike was not in good condition and it was

time for me to buy a new one. But I wasn't sure whether I should buy a hybrid again or replace it with a road bike. One of my neighbours owns a custom-built road bike and offered it to me for the ride from London to Bath. I had never tried a road bike before, believing that drop handles put too much strain on one's back. However, I decided to take her bike for a spin to help me make up my mind.

The bike had been made 20 years ago but my neighbour has kept it in good condition. I found it light and agile. But its pedals were fitted with toe clips and cage straps made of leather. She told me that all the new road bikes had strapless pedals that saved you from falling off. I enjoyed the test ride, gliding along the road on this super-light vehicle. But I thought it was too risky to borrow it for a long ride.

I use my hybrid bike as a workhorse that carries my weekly shopping on its handlebars and I like to carry my shoulder bag on the rack. For 18 years I had used only hybrid road-and-mountain bikes for commuting in London. I decided to buy a Ridgeback bike from a shop in my old neighbourhood from which I'd been buying bikes over the years. The owner of the shop knew my leg measurements and found the right-size frame for me. He adjusted the saddle so that only my toes touched the ground while I stood on it. I also got the bike fitted with a meter because I wanted to time myself on the day of the ride.

My neighbour persuaded me to buy a windcheater in case it rained on the big day. I cycled to Central London to buy this and other gear for my ride. A few big shops for cyclists had opened around Great Portland Street and I popped into one of them to buy my stuff. There were so many different kinds of Lycra shorts that I had to ask the shop assistant which of them he'd recommend for a long ride. He showed me bib shorts, which are worn by men like a woman's swimming costume. I asked him what happens when you have to go to the toilet. "You'll have to take off your jersey and then pull your bib shorts down," he replied. I decided to buy normal shorts to spare myself such a performance.

One of the perks of working in the hotel industry is that you get free access to a gym on the property. But I hadn't been inside our gym for a workout for as long as I could remember. I entered the gym to speak to one of our personal trainers and asked him for his advice. He was a great sport and a good friend. When I told him that I planned to go on a 100-mile ride, he told me in his usual jaunty manner that it would be a piece of cake – he himself having walked across Scotland. He gave me a few useful tips on how to build stamina before the ride. He suggested that I should use a rowing machine and a treadmill for half an hour three or four times a week and increase my mileage gradually on the bike before going on the ride itself. I didn't want to ride a bike in a gym. I preferred to go to a real outdoor location. So I chose to do a few laps around Regents Park before going to work at the hotel for the next couple of weeks to bring my speed to a constant 14 miles an hour.

The starting point of the ride was the Harlequins Rugby Stadium in Twickenham. I would have liked to cycle there from my home but that meant an additional 17 miles. I reckoned this would have been pushing my luck and decided to hire a cab to take me there, together with my bike.

It was still dark when we reached the stadium. On the way I saw quite a few cyclists and found a few groups of them already gathered outside the stadium. The total number of participants was only a few hundred, unlike the ride from London to Brighton, which has thousands of cyclists taking part because it's only half the distance. There were a couple of vendors selling hot breakfasts from their vans – just what many of us needed before setting off.

We received instructions about obeying traffic laws and were told that the route was signposted and there would be a handful of marshals along the route to point us in the right direction. We were also told where to stop for refreshment on the way. Looking around at the large number of well-built men and women mounted on their slim road bikes and eager to get going, I realized that you don't have to be a gym enthusiast to take part in a long bike ride – all it takes is a resolve to finish it. My purpose in taking part – to raise some money for people who had suffered a natural disaster – had given me bags of determination.

We reached the first refreshment stop before time. It was a garden centre. They were unable to open the tills before the start of their trading hours. However, they offered tea, coffee and pastries to everyone for free, and told us we could make a small donation to a good cause in a box provided on the counter. It was like meeting good Samaritans during a pilgrimage.

There wasn't much traffic on the road that Sunday morning. The route became scenic after we left densely populated southwest London behind us. If a fellow-cyclist overtook me, he or she exchanged a greeting with me. The phone in the back pocket of my jersey rang a few times. I tried to ignore it at first but then decided to pick it up after stopping at the edge of the road. While I was on the phone, the cyclists who saw me would stop and ask me if I needed any help. I thought that was great camaraderie.

I missed the pub where we were supposed to stop for lunch but then saw a group of men and women riding in a peloton – a pack of cyclists saving energy by close proximity – behind me. As they too were looking for a place to eat, we found a secluded tuck shop and stopped there. All of them had road bikes and were surprised to see me riding a hybrid. I followed their peloton during the next stage of the ride. We didn't miss the place for afternoon tea as a lot of cyclists had gathered there before hitting the home stretch. Some of them were having their bikes fixed in a mobile workshop.

Before reaching Bath, we turned off into a country road. The smell of manure was overpowering. I was eagerly waiting for the meter I had got fixed on my handlebar to register the 100th mile and felt exhilarated when the double digits became three. The last 13 miles were like unwinding after a great workout. The sight of the Royal Crescent in Bath took all my fatigue away. I saw a Japanese couple who had got there before me on their small folding bikes, which take considerably more effort to ride, and I realized that just as hybrid bikes are less efficient than road bikes, they are more robust than the smaller-wheeled folding bikes, thus making it a comparatively easy ride for me.

It wasn't until after riding a bike in London for a decade that I became aware of being a habitual cyclist. Though I had admittedly got a nod or two from fellow-cyclists on my way to work in a stationery shop in Hampstead as a reticent acknowledgment of belonging to their fraternity. A man who rode a bike and whose hair was often dishevelled came into the shop now and again to buy paper and pens. Someone told me that he was a Law Lord. I was taken aback to hear it, firstly to hear that there was such a personage as a Law Lord here in London, and secondly that he rode an old bike. In Kashmir, bicycles were used by such workmen as carpenters, masons and butchers. A carpenter and a mason usually carried their tools in a thick bag on the rack of their bike, and a butcher balanced a few slaughtered sheep, whose hides and guts had been removed, on either side of his bike. The bicycles were usually used as load-carriers and would therefore have been thought unbefitting for a highly qualified judge like a Law Lord.

The postman who delivered letters in our neighbourhood in Srinagar rode a bike with a basket fixed to its front to carry mail. However, the postmen in the old town carried a sack of letters over their shoulders and went from one shop to another to deliver them. The postman who brought letters to my father's shop wore a Khaki turban. I believed him to be a Hindu or Pandit, as they are called in Kashmir, because Muslims usually wore white turbans and I didn't realise it was part of his Khaki uniform until I heard my grandfather chatting to him about it one day.

I have known only one postman who delivered occasional letters to our home for many years, and when, after a long sojourn in London, I travelled to Srinagar I saw him working behind the counter in our local post office. I asked him about his bicycle and he told me that because he'd broken his leg in an accident some time ago he was now working at a post office counter. I was overcome with sadness since he was the one who had handed me the envelope containing my very first passport.

When I worked in a stationers in Hampstead, I met a poet who lived locally and sported a white Whitmanesque beard. He would park his bike outside the shop and walk in wearing his protective helmet. I usually had a chat with him and one day he gave me a piece of sound advice: if I ever decided to be a writer, he said, I should learn some useful skill like carpentry or plumbing to make a living. Some years later I met him again, sitting on a bench on West Hill with his helmet on as usual and his bike reclining against a wall. He told me that he had compiled a book of ballads on the theme of cycling.

I had gone straight from riding a tricycle when I was a child to riding my father's bicycle as an adolescent. It was made by Raleigh, which was the biggest cycle manufacturer in the world a century ago. I was fascinated by its head-badge logo, which depicts the head and neck of a heron standing tall above its monogram. Raleigh and its rival manufacturer, Humber, were relics of the Raj since both companies were founded in Victorian England. My father's bike weighed a ton and I couldn't reach the saddle of an adult bike. But the children who rode their father's bikes in my neighbourhood were like trapeze artists: they didn't straddle the frame but reached the adjoining paddle by pushing one leg through the frame. My father always locked his bike at home but I knew where he hid the key and often took it for a spin after he went to work, which was within walking distance.

The children in my part of town could rent an adult bike on an hourly basis from a cycle repair shop. The bikes mostly came in two colours, either black or dark green. One of the bike shops in Srinagar was run by a blind man who assessed damage by running his fingers over the faulty part. I sometimes stopped outside his shop just to watch how he fixed the bikes, feeling deep respect for him. I always feared the prospect of a rogue passing him a fake banknote. But I took comfort from an old Kashmiri saying which asserts that a blind man's wife is always under God's own wings.

European and American tourists who visited Srinagar rented bikes from a shop near Lake Dal and it was quite a common sight to see them riding along the shores of the lake mounted on a tall bike. You could spot them from far off because they wore brightly coloured windcheaters. However, there was always an odd one out who would choose to dress like a local and wear a long outer garment in winter, made of tweed. There was a professor in Kashmir University who had returned from the Sorbonne in Paris and had a bushy beard split in the middle. Because he wore casual clothes and rode a bike he was mistaken by many for a European tourist.

It wasn't uncommon, though, to invite an eccentric Englishman or a woman wearing Kashmiri clothes to your home in Srinagar if you could strike up a conversation with them on the street. I would occasionally find a tourist adrift from Lake Dal at the home of a friend, invited by his family. My friend would seek the wisdom of a guest who had visited so many lands.

Kashmir had become a popular destination during the years of the Hippie Trail when young people travelled overland from Europe to India. Long hair had become fashionable among the men involved in the Kashmir tourist trade, but the elders in Srinagar referred to the style as Happy rather than Hippie. Some of the men from Lake Dal also wore cowboy boots to appear more stylish.

While riding a bike in Kashmir, you always sat straight back on the saddle. I only once saw a bike with a drop handle. It was owned by a man who lived in our neighbourhood and ran a souvenir shop at an out-of-town tourist resort. He had perhaps bought his road bike from a tourist in exchange for goods or services. When tourists who arrived in Srinagar to stay in houseboats on Lake Dal ran out of cash, they usually sold their perfumes and cigarettes to raise some money. But it was also still possible for a penniless visitor to rely on the kindness of strangers to stay in Srinagar for a few months. When Robert, a fellow hotel worker in London, met me for the first time and came to know that I was from Kashmir, he told me that he'd spent six months in Srinagar without any money at all.

It was teachers rather than students who rode bikes to school in Srinagar. A dour retired tutor visited the home of our neighbour in the evenings to give private lessons to his children. He locked his bike in the courtyard of the house. One day a mischievous child deflated a tyre of his bike while the tutor was administering lessons and corporal punishment to his pupils. Our neighbour questioned all the children living in the vicinity the next day in a failed attempt to catch the culprit.

There were two bike repair shops in our neighbourhood. The mechanics often took bikes apart to repair them. They would even open the ball bearings and change the worn-out steel balls inside them. They wouldn't change a tube if it had a puncture but the mechanic would put a patch on it and all the tubes had several patches pasted onto them before they became unusable. Similarly, if there was a cut or hole in the tyre, the mechanic would put a piece of an old tyre inside, which gave it a slight bump. If the fork of a bike snapped, the mechanic would replace it with the fork of an old bike from his scrapyard. One ingenious mechanic replaced the handlebar of his bike with the steering wheel of a car, which impressed tourists and locals alike.

We call the fork of a bike *tongs* in Kashmiri. So when I got my first bike in London, I struggled to explain a fault to a mechanic since I wasn't familiar with the names of the individual bike-parts in English. It was a real surprise to see the mechanic replacing the tube whenever there was a puncture instead of mending it. I bought a hand pump and used it for a few years until someone told me it was a useless tool and I should buy a foot pump instead. I realised that I'd been riding a bike for a long time without realizing that its tyres were only half inflated.

If you ask bike mechanics in London to fit a new chain, they'll insist on changing the cogs of your bike as well. Otherwise you'll have to buy a chain and do it yourself. I have discovered that you can replace the chain if it's skidding and the cogs will work for a couple of years more. However, I am never sure about the alignment of the chain, which has to be measured against a centre line on an imaginary plane. I only rode single-speed bikes in Kashmir but gearless bikes seem to have become fashionable these days for people who cycle for exercise rather than for commuting. A few years ago, I carried a bike with me on a plane from London to Srinagar. Because it has gears it became an object of curiosity when I took a ride to the local shops to buy groceries. Two or three children actually asked me to show them how to change gears.

After riding a few other bikes in London I bought a Raleigh. It turned out to be a beast like my father's and weighed more than I had got accustomed to while riding my previous bikes to work. I realised it costs as much to overhaul an average bike in London as the price of a new one. I reluctantly replace my bike every four or five years, but I don't like the idea of consigning my old iron horse to a knacker's yard (otherwise known as a recycling depot) and so I usually give my old bikes to acquaintances who cycle now and again. To overhaul a bike in London after riding it every day for years means replacing everything except its frame. The wheels are thrown away if they are only slightly buckled.

I sometimes saw the blind man who ran a bike repair shop in Srinagar tightening the spokes of a wheel mounted on a stand before giving it a spin and checking with his fingers a gap of a few millimetres between the stand and the rim of the wheel to make sure it was straight. It was moving to see how he made his living. The overhauled bikes were fitted with decorative accessories such as colourful grips on the handlebar which had tassels attached to them. A tough leather saddle was wrapped in a padded foam cover to make it feel soft, just as a woollen blanket is placed on the saddle of a real horse to make it comfortable. The bikes also had a mirror fitted on the right-hand side of the handlebar. And some of the bikes had a dynamo fitted at the back to power a front light.

I thought the bicycles looked stripped to the bone when

I saw road bikes in London without chain covers, mudguards, racks and stands. It was amusing to see big men in tight-fitting Lycra riding wafer-thin bikes and carrying a load on their backs in a rucksack; some of them even wore a chain lock around their waist like a cummerbund.

A year ago, I was riding home from work as usual at midnight along Spaniards Road when I saw a long trail of cyclists riding in the opposite direction. They were out for a ride during the night with flashing lights on their bikes. Some of them had an extra light fitted to their helmet like a miner's lamp. The steady stream of cyclists didn't finish until I reached the other end of this road and stopped to give way to motorists at a blind spot. I was amused when one of the cyclists asked me if I'd lost my way, having seen me ride in the opposite direction, perhaps thinking I was a participant in his own nocturnal expedition.

In 2007, I was searching for a home in a neighbourhood that wasn't too far from Central London because I relied on a pushbike to get to the city centre. At the time I was living in a rented room on the south side of Hampstead Heath and it was only a short hop on my bike from there to the West End. However, I wasn't prepared to move far from Hampstead because of my love of the Heath.

One day, I cycled up East Heath Road and passed Jack Straw's Castle before riding along Spaniards Road, which cuts through the Heath, to explore the neighbourhood of East Finchley. It was like riding along a country lane to see a triangular traffic sign with an antlered deer painted on it, warning motorists to watch out for wild animals crossing the road.

I turned into The Bishops Avenue to reach the high street in East Finchley. It was a summer's day and I sat in a coffee shop to experience something of the local scene. A cinema in the high street was showing arthouse films. There were a couple of bike shops and a second-hand bookshop. The bookshop's window display was very enticing and I was familiar with its sister shop in Camden Lock. I liked the neighbourhood. The shops in East Finchley looked a lot more useful than the boutiques in Hampstead High Street.

It's possible that I had drawn a map in my subconscious mind to find a home within the periphery of the North Circular Road. When I spotted an advert for a small flat for sale near East End Road that was just a few hundred yards inside the orbital, I made an appointment with an agent to view it. I could hear the distant hum of the traffic on the A406 road when I reached the location. It was exactly a year before the financial crash of 2008 and prospective home-buyers were treading on each other's heels to view an available house or flat.

For over 10 years now, I have been riding along my favourite cycling route in London – the Spaniards Road – on my daily commute to work, and still find it exhilarating when I pass Whitestone Pond – one of the highest points in London – on my way back home at midnight.

❦

The Allure of Hotels

"I have every useless thing in my house… the only thing wanting is the necessary thing," recounts M. Legrandin to the young narrator in *Swann's Way* by Marcel Proust. Legrandin then tells him: "You have a soul of rare quality, an artist's nature; never let it starve for lack of what it needs." The author of *À la Recherche du Temps Perdu* always stayed at the Grand Hotel in Cabourg, where a promenade is named after him. But in Paris he frequented the Ritz, which is why some people liked to call him 'Proust of the Ritz'. He often took a room in the hotel for a few hours in order to avoid the patrons of its dining room. However, when someone referred to the room in the hotel occupied by him as 'Proust's room', he was bemused because he knew it belonged to him only in name.

When I started working in a hotel, in London in 2001, I met an elderly couple from the neighbourhood who mentioned that they chose to stay with us for a few days every year for a break, even though they had a second home in Portugal. I was as baffled to hear this as I was to find ice machines on each floor of the hotel, since I wasn't accustomed to the mixing of ice cubes in drinks.

William Morris was fond of saying "Have nothing in your house that you do not know to be useful, or believe to be beautiful." But how difficult it is in reality for most of us to part with things that we have acquired over the years, many of which are utterly pointless. A stay in a hotel not only offers us a break from the humdrum in everyday life but also provides us with a welcome opportunity to realize how very few things we actually need in order to live.

We need just a few clothes instead of wardrobes full of old garments, some of which we are never going to wear again. I arrived in the UK with a holdall bag and liked the idea of owning just two pairs of jeans and three shirts. As a youngster, I heard that an Indian Prime Minister had borrowed a jacket from a drycleaner to keep himself warm when he visited Kashmir. It wasn't clear, by the way, when someone hired a suit or jacket from a drycleaner, whether it belonged to the owner of the shop or to one of his customers who had forgotten to collect it.

It is always a good idea to travel light in life rather than carry a lot of baggage – physical as well as emotional. Even if you check into a hotel without a carry-on bag, you will find that everything needed for a good night's sleep is provided in the room. In fact, it is very liberating to live with very few things for a day or two. Thankfully, this experience is enhanced by the fact that the décor in most hotels has changed from baroque to minimalist over the course of the last century.

In the beginning, I found it disconcerting to see how

many nights a frequent business traveller spends in a hotel away from home until I learnt that Vladimir Nabokov had spent the last 16 years of his life living with his wife in the Montreux Palace Hotel. I realized then that it's possible to make a hotel your home. It doesn't astonish any more when I see someone checking into a hotel for a few days only to end up staying there for years.

When I heard a song by The Eagles for the first time, sung by a curly-haired street performer in the West End of London, I mistakenly believed that 'Hotel California' actually existed, rather than belonging to the realm of the imagination. It took me some time to understand the meaning of its last couplet:

You can check out any time you like
But you can never leave!

It finally dawned on me that when you stay often in a hotel it becomes a habit of the mind. Someone once said that men usually think of their home as a hotel whereas women can effortlessly make a hotel room look like home. It is always a pleasure to enter a hotel room whose occupant has kept it immaculate. Sometimes I find that people who stay in a hotel for a couple of weeks because they're in process of moving home have laid out their files neatly on a table top.

Hotels certainly constituted a separate moral universe – a decadent one – for my family in Kashmir. As a matter of fact, it is the restaurants that are called 'hotels' in Srinagar. I was reported to my elders by a cousin for eating out in such a restaurant when I was a teenager and found myself at a loss for many months after. I severed ties with my cousin and his family because of that. A few years later, when I travelled to Delhi and came across a few big hotels belonging to international chains, it was like finding an oasis in a desert to sit in the spacious lobby of one of these hotels and read a book.

For seven years after I moved to the UK, I often changed jobs in London, before finding work in the hospitality industry. A hotel seemed like an ideal place to work because it was full of transients like myself and I experienced it as a kind of homecoming. London appeared welcoming for the first time. I had failed to make many friends in my neighbourhood and therefore found it enchanting that you could greet a guest in the dead of night if you walked past him or her in a long hotel corridor. This was in total contrast to stealing a glance when you happened to encounter a not particularly neighbourly neighbour while walking on Hampstead Heath.

Proust had found ordinary events in the Ritz more interesting than the extraordinary events taking place in the world outside. I had intended to work in the hospitality industry in London for only a few years, but have now spent longer in a hotel than Vladimir Nabokov in his Palace Hotel – albeit as a concierge rather than a guest.

It is customary for most of our staff to stay in the hotel on Christmas Eve. For many years, though, I have resisted the temptation to stay in-house during the festive period and chosen to go home instead since I can come to work by bike as usual on Christmas Day when there is no public transport. However, there was one occasion when I decided to stay in the hotel to mark the end of a busy year and it turned out to be a pleasant surprise.

I was allocated a sample refurbished room, a room I was familiar with because I'd shown it to many visitors in order to obtain preliminary customer feedback regarding a general refurbishment planned for the New Year. Now it was time for me to find out for myself what it was like to stay in such a room.

It felt bigger than a standard room because the wardrobe had been removed and replaced with an open storage frame for clothes and shoes. A flat-screen TV was mounted on the wall, with a bench placed under it for luggage instead of a big chest of drawers, and a section of the wall where there had once been a desk was now covered with a full-length mirror reflecting the headboard of the bed and the painting mounted next to it, which virtually doubled the width of the room. A sturdy round table near the bed, with a stylish lounge chair on one side and an armchair made of solid metal on the other, functioned as a work area. The subdued colour of the wallpaper appeared quite Zen-like in the diffused light of swing-arm lamps. The new beds weren't covered with valance drapery, which made the room look neater, nor did they have castor wheels, which meant that the beds wouldn't move if slightly pushed.

Staying overnight in a new room made me realise how

much thought had gone into its design. The hotel chain has a design lab at its headquarters where ideas are tested before a design for a guest room is finalised. As I moved back and forth from this room into other guest rooms during the evening, it dawned on me how our guests' expectations had changed in the last few years.

The previous refurbishment had been in 2007 when the iPhone 1 was first released in America. Since then, the technology has become central to how we explore and make sense of the world. Most of us now carry various gadgets while travelling and need to charge more than one device during our stay in a hotel. I found multiple USB ports for the charging of phones and tablets in the new room, which meant that guests didn't need to carry universal adaptors with them to power up their devices.

The mini-bar had been replaced with a fridge, which is more customer-friendly than miniature drinks lined up on sensors that automatically charge you for consumption. An elephant made out of orange wire mesh rested on top of the fridge to remind the guests of the hotel's proximity to London Zoo. The hairdryer hung in open view by the mirror instead of being hidden away in a drawer (I am often asked by guests if there is a hairdryer in the room). In the bathroom the bath had been replaced by a walk-in shower, which made it more convenient for those guests who couldn't step in and out of the bath. A picture frame in the bathroom had a City of Westminster sign from a bygone era placed within it, which stated, 'Please adjust your dress before leaving'. It somehow reminded me that an old-fashioned lady who came to the hotel now and again always asked me if she could use 'the powder room' in the hotel lobby rather than, more explicitly, 'the ladies toilet'.

It is a peculiar feeling when you become a guest instead of a hotel staff member for a day in the hotel where you work. You want to wash the used cups in the room instead of leaving it for the room attendants to wash them for you. Although I worked on the same wage as my colleagues in the housekeeping department, a friend corrected me when I told him that I work at 'the bottom rung of the ladder' in the hospitality industry. He reminded me that the physical labour of the men and women cleaners is tougher than a concierge's. His words resounded in my head so forcefully that I felt compelled to empty the rubbish bin in my room and take it to the compactor before I checked out.

*

How did it come about that I found myself working in what is called The Hospitality Industry? That had not been my plan. My prior work experience in London had been somewhat different.

In September 2000 I was desperately looking for a job when I spotted a notice displayed in a bookshop in Central London advertising a temporary vacancy for a bookseller. I had always thought that a bookshop would be an ideal place to work in but a bookselling job had so far eluded me.

I submitted my CV along with a covering letter expressing my unfaltering love of literature. I was called in for an interview the next day. The bookshop was very busy as it was the beginning of the academic year and, in addition to its general sales, the shop stocked textbooks for college students.

It was an easy interview. The interviewer didn't ask me any troublesome questions. I was lucky that she didn't ask me which title I would recommend if someone wanted to buy a book for their 9-year-old nephew. At that time I'd never heard of Harry Potter.

I was offered a job until Christmas that year and happily accepted it. The Human Resources (HR) manager handed me a badge with just a logo of the shop on it, which looked cool. No uniform was provided but all the booksellers wore the same colour T-shirt.

I was sent to work in the basement of this big bookshop and I got on well with the staff there. They fondly called themselves The Basement Gang. When the man who took me on an introductory tour of my section told me that he liked to read Nabokov and Proust we immediately became friends. As a new recruit, I was assigned to work behind the till rather than answering the queries of university students and their tutors. One of the staff members there had such a prodigious memory that she knew the multiple-digit ISBN numbers of many titles by heart. I drifted into other sections of this great bookshop during my lunch breaks and got to know the sales staff. On one of the upper floors an erudite staff member called Mr Khan showed me his section and explained how he separated History from Politics titles on the shelves.

The bookshop buzzed during the Christmas season. Three months passed very quickly and I hoped for a miracle that would enable me to carry on working there after the New Year. Then I heard that someone who worked in the basement section was planning to leave. Having worked there myself during a busy period, I felt optimistic that I would get this job. But I was surprised to learn that I'd have to go through another interview if I wanted a permanent position.

The lady from the HR department, whom I had seen occasionally on the shop floor, was accompanied by a senior manager who had the reputation of being somewhat stringent. In fact, she was the one who started asking me questions this time around about my previous jobs. Indeed, she asked me a question which many employers think is central to a job interview – where did I see myself in five years' time?

I replied that I wanted to save some money and buy a lot of books before starting work on writing my own book. With hindsight, I'm convinced that it was these words that sealed my fate. Sure enough, I learnt a couple of days later that my application had failed. Not only that, my existing job would end in a week's time.

Although I was heartbroken, I didn't regret that I'd told my interviewer the truth. Perhaps she would have preferred to hear that I wanted to follow in her footsteps and be put in charge of one of the basement sections of the shop. Anyway, my colleagues were sorry to see me leave and gave me a farewell card and a copy of *The Writer's Handbook* as a parting gift.

I was back in the market for a job, and a friend who thought it might suit my disposition suggested that I should look for a job in the hospitality industry. I sent my CV to a few hotels, including one in my own neighbourhood that had recently undergone refurbishment and was looking for a concierge. Since I had roamed the streets of Central London on my bike for many years and knew the location of theatres, museums and galleries, I thought this experience would help me pass the job interview. I had read a letter by Marcel Proust to one of his friends in which he described the Ritz hotel in Paris as 'a desert without an oasis' when a concierge is off sick, alluding to a line from Baudelaire's 'Le Voyage'*: 'Une oasis d'horreur dans un désert d'ennui'.* I also liked the idea of Nabokov making the Montreux Palace hotel his permanent home.

I arrived at the hotel midmorning and told the concierge on duty that I was there for a job interview. An amiable Cypriot, he welcomed me to the hotel. One of the Reception managers soon appeared. He sat me down in the bar and offered me a coffee. I couldn't help remembering my unsuccessful bookshop interview two months before, conducted in a dingy room.

Fortunately, the Reception manager did not ask me the infamous question, 'Where do you see yourself in five years' time?' I would have replied 'probably dead'. At the end of the interview I was asked if there was anything I'd like to ask him. I asked whether I could work a few extra shifts on top of my contracted hours if I was offered the job. He said he didn't see why not, which cheered me up.

I still frequented the bookshop in Central London every week to browse and buy the books I liked, and three years later I started work on the manuscript of my own book. The book launch party took place at the hotel and I invited a few of my old colleagues from the bookshop. It was a friend from the bookshop whom I asked to read an excerpt since he has a melodious voice.

*

I sometimes sat with a book in the lobby of Le Méridien to escape the oppressive heat of New Delhi in summer. It was considered an extravagance by the elders in my family to drink a coffee in a plush hotel and therefore I never set foot in the coffee shop of Le Méridien. When one of my cousins, who had tea with his fiancée in the café, told my aunt the price, she thought it most ostentatious of him to entertain his betrothed there.

One day I went up in the glass lift to see the room of a friend who was visiting from Europe together with his neighbour. The high floor offered a panoramic view of Edwin Lutyen's grandly designed Delhi, and my friends were surprised to see that the hotel was surrounded by trees as far as the eye could see. They had expected the city to be teeming only with people.

In 2009, after a long absence, I visited Kashmir for the second time in a year. It was cold and hazy in Srinagar in November. Many people had put on their winter gear and the town seemed less crowded than heretofore. I relied on my friends and family to drive me around the town as they thought it wasn't a good idea for me to ride a pushbike in Srinagar.

The drive around Lake Dal offered a resplendent view of Srinagar, in contrast to the clutter of the old town. It was the sight of this lake that caused a poet to say, when he arrived in the town from a village five centuries ago, that there was a whiff of paradise in the air. The lake must have been pristine then but today its colour is green because of the weeds that grow in it.

A few old friends had arranged to meet me in the garden of the Grand Palace Hotel for a coffee. It was built as a Maharaja's home a century ago and had become a hotel after he left Kashmir. The hotel had changed hands recently and was now run by another chain. Our car was stopped by an armed security guard who politely asked us the purpose of our visit. The lobby of the Grand Palace was very quiet. There was a candle burning by the portrait of the late owner of this hotel chain who had died of a heart attack in a hospital in London. The receptionist told us that occupancy of the hotel was very low and he was trying to get transferred to another branch outside the state of Jammu and Kashmir. We decided to sit outside in the garden to have tea. The garden café offered a limited menu since the hotel was quiet. However, sitting in the garden of the Grand Palace was a pleasure in itself since it offered us a chance to catch the sunset over the mountains at the other end of the Vale of Kashmir. The peace and tranquillity this place offered made me forget that I was in Srinagar.

As a child, I was intrigued by the permanent 'To Let' signs hung at the front of every houseboat. The reflection of two footlights on each boat in the water of the lake made them look very enticing in the evening. A white-bearded man sold woollen caps made in Srinagar and cigarettes made by the British American Tobacco Company, like Benson & Hedges and Dunhill, on his colourful cart on the Boulevard. These cigarettes were bought and sold by the foreign tourists in Srinagar. He also sold toiletries with barcodes printed on them which – without knowing the actual function of the barcodes – he showed to his clients as proof that those products weren't made in India. I was also baffled by signboards on the frontage of shops and restaurants on the Boulevard which featured such words as 'Objets d'art', 'Curios' and 'Continental Breakfast'.

It was only when I started to work in a hotel in London that I realised that the typical English Breakfast meant a fry-up whereas the Continental Breakfast is of a lighter kind, which is why some of the hotels like to call it a Healthy Option Breakfast. When an American guest requested more teabags, I asked him if he would like English Breakfast or Earl Grey. He quipped that there is no such thing as an English tea, which is grown either in Assam or Darjeeling. I thought he had a point and conceded my defeat. When I saw the Full English Breakfast laid out on a buffet, I understood why some people still regard breakfast as the most important meal of the day.

The restaurant in Srinagar, which advertised 'Continental Breakfast' on its signboard and was frequented by foreign tourists, had a white interior and the tables were covered with white linen. The houseboats on neighbouring Lake Dal had their own kitchens at the back and employed men from a certain village in Kashmir who could cook delectable food for Sahibs and Memsahibs visiting Kashmir. The wives of the houseboat owners cooked the sort of mild food that suits the European and American palate. I got to taste their food when a man from Lake Dal who ran a souvenir shop in New Delhi shared the food from his home with two or three French tourists and a couple of other people who happened to be in his shop at lunchtime. He said that French people liked to eat rice when, not so long ago, they used to visit Lake Dal in droves – it now seemed quite a distant era. Among the domestic tourists staying in his houseboat were Bengalis who, like the French, loved to eat rice. He categorised the French as rice 'Firangis' – a term of endearment in Srinagar for a European or American tourist, though during the Raj era it implied an attitude of hostility in various towns in the Indian subcontinent.

The houseboat owners also arranged a cook or Khansama, as they liked to call them, to accompany Firangi guests on trekking expeditions. Thus, working in the hospitality industry in Kashmir meant working as a chef rather than anything else. There was a hotel management school overlooking the Dal that trained students from other parts of the Valley to work in hotels outside Kashmir, rather than pointlessly train the sons of houseboat owners who had the tourist business ingrained in them from an early age. The Sanskrit saying, 'Atithi Devo Bhava', means that a guest is akin to God, but for the dweller of Lake Dal a guest was the Deity himself. It is because Sanskrit underlies the Indo-European languages that I had thought the Kashmiri language was derived from Sanskrit until a guest at the hotel told me that, on the contrary, Kashmiri originates from Sharda, which is considered to be the mother of Sanskrit.

*

As someone who is naturally shy, I wasn't cut out to work in the hospitality industry. A few weeks after I started working in a hotel, a woman from Florida who had stayed there for two or three weeks embraced me warmly in the lobby and said, "We Americans like to show our emotions". I felt moved to see tears in her eyes. The chilly world I had got accustomed to while living in the neighbourhood of the hotel suddenly changed to one of conviviality. A group of Jazz musicians arrived soon after from New Orleans to play at a nearby venue and they were full of life and made the lobby of our hotel resound with their laughter.

I heard the use of the word 'incognito' for the first time while working in a hotel. It is commonly used in the hospitality industry to describe a guest who likes to be invisible and doesn't want anyone to know that he or she is staying there. For instance, I spotted an accomplished filmmaker living in the hotel for weeks on end and later came to learn that his marriage had broken down, which is why he chose to live in a hotel. An actor who played tough-guy roles in films and TV series told me once that he was falling to pieces because he was going through a divorce. His frank admission evoked feelings of deep sympathy in me. And one day a lady who looked very upset slapped her husband in the lobby of the hotel and told me that he was involved with a woman who was the same age as their daughter. He spent his monthly salary on her instead of paying their mortgage instalments and they had now run into arrears. She said that she held a doctoral degree in science and felt deeply ashamed about her husband having an affair. The husband stood there with his head bowed. Nonetheless, I saw that his face was bruised, but his silence belied his innocent expression.

It was also while working in a hotel that I heard for the first time a person who wasn't a regular guest described as a transient. Someone once remarked that I was drawn to work in a hotel in London because hotels are transient places. Perhaps there's a certain truth in that as I had felt disenchanted by my life in London and found the hotel to be a kind of oasis – the Baudelaire allusion again – in an otherwise barren landscape.

I was hardly ever invited to a wedding during my

first seven years in London. But I have been invited to a few weddings since I started working in a hotel. An elegant lady whom I mistook for someone I had seen on television asked me for a favour one afternoon at the hotel. She wanted me to be a witness at her son's wedding ceremony in a town hall in Camden. I obliged because she didn't know many people in London. A few years later, another guest insisted that I attend the wedding of his daughter in the same town hall.

I reached the town hall before the appointed time to discover the writer V. S. Naipaul in a wheelchair in an anteroom waiting for the bride and groom to arrive. I greeted him with a nod. Noticing the bouquet that I held, he asked me if I was there to attend the same wedding ceremony. His wife told me that he liked to be punctual. The last time I had seen Naipaul was in 2001 – the year I started to work in a hotel – at a literary festival in Cheltenham. He had walked to the podium quite easily so it was sad to see him this time reliant on a wheelchair.

A few minutes later, Naipaul asked me how I knew the couple who were to be married. I told him that I was working in a hotel where the parents of the bride were guests. I suddenly remembered his talk at the festival a decade and a half before when he said that if someone stopped him in the street to sell him an insurance policy, he would like to know about the man. His curiosity about the world and its inhabitants was undiminished even though he relied on a carer to assist him with his mobility.

My job in a hotel inspired me to travel again after being somewhat bogged down in London for many years. I often met people from faraway places who stayed in the hotel, a few of whom weren't even fit to travel. I thought I had no excuse for not roaming the British Isles and Continental Europe before I got to my own third act. Once I met an elderly guest in the lobby of the hotel who seemed to be lost. He asked me if he was in Paris or in London. There seemed to be no point in asking him for his room number. This prompts me to recall a phrase made famous by a TV documentary about a party of Americans on a whirlwind package tour of Europe. When a bewildered tourist asks another in the party what country they're in, her fellow-tourist replies, "If it's Tuesday, it must be Belgium."

It is the names of hotels more than any other venues that evoke sweet memories of the past in some of us. I often hear people saying that they stayed in a certain hotel when they got married and it's like a homecoming for them to stay in that hotel again. I well remember ordering a cup of tea as a schoolboy in the restaurant of a hotel in a mountain resort in Kashmir for the first time. The waiter brought a pot of tea instead and told me that they didn't sell tea by the cup. I was impressed to see that they took the ritual of serving tea in a restaurant of a hotel so seriously as I was only familiar with roadside tea-stalls until then. The name of that hotel remains imprinted in my mind. It derived from a type of flower that grows wild in the cemeteries of Srinagar, and therefore some people in Kashmir like to call it *fleur-de-cimetière*. The tables in that restaurant were covered in white linen cloths like the ones in the restaurant near Lake Dal where I saw mostly foreign tourists having their meals. It was a bedazzling experience for me to order a tea in such a restaurant, as if I had entered a magical world through a secret door of a kind that only exists in children's stories.

Years later, in my early twenties, I borrowed a car and some money from a friend in Delhi to invite a woman I happened to meet by chance on the road for high tea in the restaurant of a renowned hotel in the town. The restaurant was called Rendezvous and I felt lucky to have a rendezvous there with a sophisticated woman from Delhi. Although I never saw her again, that day has lingered in my memory ever since. Proust goes as far as saying that the resurrection of the soul may be conceived as a phenomenon of memory.

Notes from Underground

I occasionally ride the Underground in London. However, it took me many trips to learn how to hold a newspaper steadily in my hands in a moving train. I was astonished to see men and women standing in a tube train carriage while holding a newspaper or open book in one hand and a briefcase or bag in the other. To my further surprise I found that most commuters on the Underground habitually keep their heads down and some of them nod off before reaching their destination. The atmosphere is always sullen inside a tube train carriage. At least it used to be entertaining to travel by tube late at night before the drinking of alcohol was banned by Transport for London in 2008. I once boarded a northbound train at midnight in the West End and saw a man staggering around, holding an empty beer can as a pretend microphone and announcing, "Ladies and gentleman, we are underground." He was deadly serious but no one in the carriage paid the slightest attention to him.

If I don't find any newspapers to read on the Tube, I gaze at the adverts on cards displayed in a long row above the carriage windows. On one occasion I was captivated by a poem printed on one of these cards. Written by Moniza Alvi, it was called 'Arrival 1946'.

> The boat docked in at Liverpool.
> From the train Tariq stared
> at an unbroken line of washing
> from the North West to Euston.
> These are strange people, he thought –
> an Empire, and all this washing,
> the underwear, the Englishman's garden.
> It was Monday, and very sharp.

This poem evokes familiar feelings in me whenever I arrive at Heathrow airport, travel by cab to my home via the North Circular Road, and see unbroken rows of houses, some of which are quite dilapidated, along the peripheral road.

Ever since I saw Alvi's poem on display, whenever I catch a train I usually walk through a few carriages in search of a Poem on the Underground. In fact it has been more than 30 years since the Poems on the Underground project began. It was the idea of an America writer, Judith Chernaik, to bring poetry to passengers who travel on the Underground. The total number of people who use the London Underground in a year currently stands at 1.3 billion, which is equivalent to the entire population of India. Judith had followed in the footsteps of her compatriot, Sam Wanamaker, who was responsible for the recreation of Shakespeare's Globe at Bankside in London.

Shakespeare's sonnets feature regularly in the Poems

on the Underground. I mentioned one such sonnet to a Hampstead woman of my acquaintance and she asked me what the number of that particular sonnet was, presumably to show her familiarity with the works of the Bard. And when I read Yeats's poem, 'Her Anxiety', on the Tube I was so overwhelmed by it that I forgot to get off at my stop.

> Earth in beauty dressed
> Awaits returning spring.
> All true love must die,
> Alter at the best
> Into some lesser thing.
> Prove that I lie.

An evocation of a Caribbean seascape by Derek Walcott can brighten a journey through a dark tunnel in subterranean London. I have also enjoyed reading many anonymous poems on the Underground. And I like to read poems that have been translated into English from Gaelic and other languages. One day I was pleased to see the poem of a fellow Kashmiri on display:

> The moon did not become the sun.
> It just fell on the desert
> in great sheets, reams
> of silver handmade by you.

As an adolescent in Kashmir I was accustomed to reading poems handwritten in decorative Urdu inside buses. The words posted above the windscreen always stated that the bus belonged to God. However, there was a kind of poetry that, as a teenager, I found rather suggestive. It appeared above passenger seats inside the buses, and it would have been embarrassing for me to quote one of these couplets in the classroom.

The Poems on the Underground project is funded by the Arts Council. I usually look out for its logo when I search for a poem among the adverts for cheap phone calls and food ordering services. I like the idea of unorthodox writers being read 'underground'. Many poems on the cards are about what it means to be a poet.

The original literal map of the Underground was floral in shape. It was Harry Beck who made it linear – and hence more legible – in his iconic design. Transport for London prints millions of handy Tube maps based on Beck's original design, apparently unaware, however, that many passengers are unable to read the names of the stations in such small print.

These days, some of the lines of the London Underground run for twenty-four hours at weekends. During my first few years in London, whenever I caught the last train home from the West End I felt regret at having spent so many evening hours in central London. It was only after I started using a bike that I discovered other facets of this great city.

Many of the Underground stations in London aren't accessible to wheelchair users or those who travel with babies in prams. A few years ago I was travelling with my little boy, who was in a pushchair, and boarded the train at an overground station near my home. When I reached my stop in central London, the platform was so deep underground that I asked a staff member for help. She advised me to ride the escalator, which was so steep that I asked her if it was safe to do so with the pushchair. She replied that many people used the same escalator with double buggies and showed me how to hold the pushchair by pressing the front-wheels against a riser on the escalator.

When I cycle home from work at midnight I usually see a group of workmen on the route in bright orange overalls, standing next to heavy equipment. They are waiting for the network to close so they can start their maintenance of the tracks in Hampstead, the deepest Underground station in London. I cycle up a winding road and cross by Whitestone Pond – London's highest point, which happens to lie halfway between my place of work and my home. Perhaps one day I will find one of the *Bike Ballads* by John Hands in the Tube. That would certainly boost my spirits.

*

As one descends into subterranean London by escalator, colourful posters carry you into a fantasy world that is far richer than the world above ground. As if by magic, a theatrical world opens before your eyes, since every other poster advertises a play or a musical. Such an experience carries me back to the days of my childhood when, at a fair, children were offered an optical instrument with a slot at the front through which pictures of far-off lands were inserted. The persistence of the impression after a luminous image is withdrawn creates the illusion of a moving picture.

The images on London Underground posters become almost life-size when you reach a platform. The artworks in the museums and galleries in London depicted on some of these posters liven up the Underground, as well as informing commuters what's on in town. I usually walk to the end of the platform to avoid the crowd in the middle and look at the posters lining the curvature of the tunnel. There is no joy to be had in travelling by train through a dark tunnel except to be dazzled by posters when you reach a platform. A friend who has visited Moscow tells me that despite impressively monumental architecture, the complete absence of advertising in the Moscow Underground ensures a certain solemnity that made him feel surprisingly deprived.

I was myself surprised to see how quickly hordes of passengers exit the carriage when the doors slide open and a jumble of commuters strive to step on board. It takes practice not to get trapped between the automatic doors. London's residential neighbourhoods struck me as rather quiet and I didn't see a mass of people in the town until I took a tube train to the West End and found the huddled humanity missing from suburban streets, everyone apparently lost in their own thoughts. This was before the advent of smart phones. Nowadays, it's commonplace to see commuters listening to music using earphones or playing games to while away the time.

Although the Underground station nearest to where I lived in Hampstead was Belsize Park, I had asked a relative who was visiting from Kashmir to meet me outside Hampstead (High Street) station. I wanted to walk home with him across the Heath towards Parliament Hill so that he could see London from a panoramic vantage point. But he wasn't accustomed to such a long walk and later told my folks in Kashmir that it had been a kind of punishment for him to walk from an Underground station to my home through vast tracts of grassland.

I have only once taken the stairs instead of a lift at Hampstead tube station. The descent down this spiral staircase seems to be never-ending, rather like being trapped in perpetuity inside a grimly constructed helix. The Northern Line emerges from the tunnel only one stop after Hampstead, at Golders Green, which is depicted as a sunny suburban idyll on a vintage Underground poster of 1905. A mother is shown reclining in a garden chair while her little girl plays on the grass and her husband waters the sunflowers. The caption on the poster reads

'Tis pleasant, through the loopholes of retreat,
To peep at such a world; to see the stir
Of the great Babel, and not feel the crowd.

This scarcely applies nowadays, since Golders Green has become a crowded neighbourhood, and its residents tell me that they breathe traffic fumes rather than fresh air as the town centre is such a busy transport hub. In addition to the many buses in transit in the yard outside the tube station, there is a National Express stop and big coaches pull up there day and night on their way from Central London to various destinations in the north of the country. Golders Green does have the advantage, however, of lying within walking distance of Hampstead Heath.

I have often cycled to Golders Green and was amused when I first heard the name 'Childs Hill', not yet knowing that it had taken its name from a landowner called Richard le Child. I'd assumed it was just a low hill that even a child could climb. I was similarly amused when I discovered a vantage point in Greenwich Park called One Tree Hill.

These days I learn more about the London Underground from my small son who is fascinated by it. He recently asked me which is the least used London Tube station and I had no answer for him. I might have guessed the busiest station, but I must confess that I have never given much thought to the question of the quietest station in such a vast network.

I cannot separate fact from fiction or folklore when it comes to the Underground since there are so many references to it in books, such as Seamus Heaney's *District and Circle*, and films, from *Hidden City* to *Skyfall*. As for folklore, consider Mornington Crescent, which for many years was closed for renovations. Someone I knew in Camden told me that this station had been used as a base by secret service agents – an implausibility that I attribute to his love of spy thrillers.

There were no trains in Kashmir during my childhood and if a school friend travelled outside the Valley with his or her family, the first question we asked when they returned was whether they had taken a ride on a train. As an adult, it was considered a rite of passage to ride in an unreserved carriage, euphemistically called a 'General Compartment' by the Indian Railways, in a train from Jammu to Delhi. Such carriages were always packed with men, women and children, plus their belongings. My uncle and I once boarded an unreserved carriage in an overnight train that was so crammed with passengers that some of them even sat in the lavatory. When I finally travelled on my own in a train from Delhi to Jammu I preferred to cling on at the carriage entrance, hanging half inside and half outside the carriage. It stirred up a small storm of dust as it passed through the clusters of makeshift houses that cropped up on both side of the tracks.

As a child, I had seen pictures of trains in my schoolbooks but not yet heard of the book entitled *The Railway Children*. In our class we sang rhymes in Urdu based on the 'chhuk-chhuk' rhythms of trains. I had also heard about double-decker buses plying some routes in Bombay and asked friends who had been there a silly question: Does the driver of a double-decker bus sit on the upper or lower deck? Some years later, a few double-decker buses were brought to Kashmir to run on a scenic route along Lake Dal. These buses couldn't be used on other routes as they were deemed too high to pass under the electricity and telephone cables that criss-cross the roads in the old town. As for double-decker trains, I had to wait until I travelled to Germany to board one of those for the first time.

Visitors to London become wide-eyed when they see a mouse running back and forth on the blackened floor of the track. However, Londoners are unfazed by such a sight, knowing that one is never far from a mouse wherever you live – and dine out – in this city. I could sometimes hear a mouse running in the hollow of the ceiling in the house in Hampstead where I lived. One day I saw a tiny mouse standing on hind legs in the corridor when I switched on the light during the night. My flatmate named it Charlie and told me, "This is London. You can't escape mice, even in the Palace of Westminster."

The quality of air in the Underground is said to be far worse than that at street level. I can't help but wonder about the days when Underground trains were pulled by coke-burning steam engines and smoking was permitted at the stations. It is quite an ordeal to travel by tube during a swelteringly hot summer. A few years ago, a fragrance wishfully called 'Madeleine' was trialled in one or two London Underground stations to make travelling more agreeable for passengers, since smell can evoke pleasant memories. But *la madeleine de Proust* had the opposite effect of making some passengers feel sick. However, it is the screeching sound that impacts on me the most when I travel by tube. Sometimes I see a sensitive commuter who cannot tolerate that level of noise covering his or her ears like the desperate figure in Edvard Munch's painting, 'The Scream'.

The story of the London Underground is intertwined with the history of the British Empire. It began in 1851 when London hosted the Great Exhibition in Hyde Park. The purpose of the exhibition was to show off the industrial prowess of Great Britain as well as to display the wealth looted from the colonies. The fabled Kohinoor diamond was on display at the exhibition, acquired just a year before under the punitive Treaty of Lahore. The Great Exhibition was organised by the Prince Consort, Albert, among others. A temporary exhibition hall made of iron and glass was built in Hyde Park and it became known as the Crystal Palace. It was also referred to by some as The Great Shalimar, alluding to the Shalimar Garden in Lahore. There is a garden in Srinagar by the same name and I liked to cycle there along the shore of Lake Dal whenever I fancied going for a long ride.

The Great Exhibition proved to be a crowd-puller, attracting 6 million visitors out of a total population at that time of 18 million Brits. The need for a mass transit system within London was felt more than ever because it often took less time to journey to London by train from the coast than reaching the West End from a train station by a horse-drawn cab. The world's first underground railway opened 12 years later, in 1863, between Paddington and Farringdon. At this time the trains were powered by steam engines. In 2013, to celebrate the 150th anniversary of the Underground, Transport for London ran a steam train again. You could still see the arched roof of a platform at Baker Street, blackened by soot.

The Crystal Palace in Hyde Park was dismantled after the exhibition and resurrected near Sydenham Hill in South London. I could see a tall TV transmitter tower at this location while standing at the top of Parliament Hill in Hampstead. It looks like the Eiffel Tower from afar. But I used to imagine an arched façade of the Crystal Palace existing near its base until I learned that the original glass structure had actually burnt to the ground in the 1930s. I have only once ventured as far as Sydenham on the other side of London. It seems like another county because Underground stations in South London are few and far between, compared to North London.

The Metropolitan Railway Company, which ran the first Underground train, has lent its name to one of the eleven lines London currently operates, and its shortened form, 'Metro', was later adopted as a name for the underground railway network in Paris – *Chemin de fer métropolitain*. Art nouveau signs bearing the word 'Métropolitain' can still be seen outside some Paris station entrances.

Since the railway locomotives were made in Britain, many of them were sold abroad to her colonies in Asia and Africa. Thousands of labourers were sent from India to East Africa to work on the building of the railways. The British Parliament passed acts to incorporate the railway companies in India and elsewhere, and for the acquisition of land to build railroads in various colonial cities.

*

When I first arrived in London and started using the Underground, I found the glazed exterior of the station buildings and their semicircular windows somewhat odd. For some reason the oxblood tiles have an uneven surface texture. Some of the station buildings had many floors added to them later in such a mishmash of styles that the Metro station entrances in Paris seem decorous by comparison.

I wondered which gap was being referred to when I first heard the announcement 'Mind the gap'. It made sense to me only when I eventually heard the full announcement: 'Mind the gap between the train and the platform'. When they make an announcement on board a ten-year-old Metro train in Dubai, it sounds very familiar: a distinct echo of the London Underground version as delivered in the well-spoken tone of a professional actor. I think one would need to take intensive elocution lessons to successfully impersonate such an announcer.

It was my son who informed me that the circle-and-bar logo of the Underground is called a 'roundel'. I had thought that a roundel was a poem of eleven lines in three stanzas. Although, in the course of my work, I often draw this logo on a piece of paper while giving directions to visitors to London, it had never occurred to me till then that this well-known logo had a name. It also took me a while to learn that the

London Underground uses its own sans-serif font, known as 'Johnston', on its signs and posters. I certainly like the idea of a public transport body commissioning works of art. During the 1930s and 1940s London Transport commissioned works by émigré artists who had fled Nazi Germany for the UK, and they produced some distinctive posters for the network.

Only recently I learnt that Harry Beck, who designed the now iconic Underground map, lived in my own neighbourhood in London. Beck was a draughtsman who designed the Underground map in his spare time as if it were the diagram of an electric circuit. Clear as it is, it isn't rendered to scale, which is perhaps why many visitors to London board certain Underground trains that travel a mere 300 metres from one station to another.

I was horror-struck to learn that, on average, 50 people throw themselves under tube trains and die each year. But you seldom find these incidents reported in the newspapers unless it's someone like a Punjabi woman who is a victim of domestic violence and has thrown herself under a train in Ealing or Southall.

Smoking in the Underground was banned seven years before I came to London. However, I was unaware precisely where the 1987 fire at King's Cross station had started (ignited by a lit match) that killed dozens of people, until someone recently pointed out to me a small plaque commemorating those who had lost their lives. A relative of mine who was accustomed to smoking in public places in Kashmir, wanted to smoke on a bus during his visit to London. When he was stopped by an aunt who was showing him around town, he responded by saying "Stop being so English". His words brought to mind the strapline from an advert for a Swedish furniture firm hoping to persuade the English to buy their modern designs.

Although the Tube is overcrowded and overpriced, most visitors and some Londoners still think it is marvellous. An American guest who was visiting London from Washington DC told me, "It's great to have such a wonderful public transport system in a big city like London. Our own government won't invest in a public transport system for Washington DC, our capital city." In fact, the London Underground currently receives a grant of 700 million pounds from the government, and the revenue generated from its advertising estate goes into improving the network.

When you take a seat in an old Tube train carriage, it sinks like a puffed up cushion. Looking at the repetitive design on the upholstery can make you dizzy so it's little wonder that some people fall asleep in their seats. One of the commonly used patterns is called 'Barman'. You'd need a microscope, though, to discover the landmarks of London depicted in it. Transport for London's ethos is to choose a design fit for purpose, not for its aesthetic value alone. Leslie Green used a William Morris motif on the ceramic tiles in some of the London Tube stations; but Morris's principle, that the beauty and utility of objects should go hand in hand in object design, hasn't been adhered to by the designers who shaped this network.

The Tube's tannoy announcements might be voiced by a typically English-sounding actor but many of its staff members are of Caribbean heritage. In fact, during the 1950s the London Underground set up recruitment centres in Barbados to find men and women who could drive its trains and run the stations.

The actual extent of the hardships suffered by Caribbean people in the UK have come to light only recently, when it was revealed that the Home Office had rejected the applications for citizenship of hundreds of West Indians who had lived and worked in the UK for half a century. Some of Clapham South's deep-level shelters of World War II, which belong to the Underground, were used to house post-war migrants from the West Indies. At a London art gallery I saw a poster commissioned by the Underground called 'Migrants of London'. It depicted migratory birds in a pond in Regents Park. The illustration celebrated their *joie de vivre* in the very heart of London, conveying the message that there are no visas or borders in the natural world.

Whereas most commuters walk hurriedly past them, I like to listen to buskers playing or singing in the Underground walkways leading to the platform. Some of these buskers have stopped me in my tracks, compelling me to listen to their music for minutes on end. Busking was tolerated in the Underground when I started using it but now you have to apply for a licence and there are strictly designated pitches. Musicians have written songs about both the sounds and stations of the Tube. Legend has it that even Paul McCartney has busked in the Underground in disguise.

Entertainment has long been associated with the London Underground. For instance, before television became popular in the 1950s, people living in the suburbs would stream into the West End in the evenings for the entertainment on offer in cinemas, theatres, and concert halls. Many writers have been inspired by the London Underground. Seamus Heaney, for instance, has composed a poem called 'The Underground' in which he imagines losing his bride if he looks back like Orpheus in quest of Eurydice, lost in the Underworld of Hades.

Bared and tensed as I am, all attention
For your step following and damned if I look back

Doris Lessing has written in defence of the Underground in her book, *London Observed*. I met her by chance two decades ago at a Hampstead stationers where I worked as a shop assistant. Doris Lessing's book *Mara and Dann* had been published a few months earlier and I had seen her photo in a newspaper. When she came to the shop counter and expressed her liking for a certain type of pen, I asked her hesitantly if it was her and she replied softy, "That's right".

Doris Lessing had come to England in 1949 from Southern Rhodesia with the manuscript of her first novel,

The Grass is Singing, which is about the relationship between a white farmer's wife and their native servant. In those days, women in the UK who married Africans were ostracized. Lessing describes London during her first year there as a kind of nightmare city. But she subsequently observed: 'Then one evening, walking across the park, the light welded buildings, trees and scarlet buses into something familiar and beautiful, and I knew myself to be at home.'

Doris Lessing was a prolific writer. I asked her if she was working on a new book and she replied, "I am always writing. Always!" And when I mentioned that we might be reading electronic books in the near future, she said, "We should resist them tooth and nail."

The bus network in London is very extensive and buses carry more people each year than the Underground. But if you are looking up an address in London, you often search for the nearest Underground station. It is always desirable to live close to a station in London. I lived in Muswell Hill for a year, a neighbourhood that isn't served by a station, and it felt like being marooned on a desert island. I often cycled for a mile and a half and locked my bike outside Highgate Wood to take a Tube train to the West End. There is a disused train station in Muswell Hill and people living in the neighbourhood who know about it are understandably regretful that it's not actively connected to the Underground network.

Incidentally, it baffles me when someone describes a woman's face as looking like "the back end of a bus".

I have always found the rounded rear end of a Routemaster bus alluring.

Since I rely more on my bike to get around London, I thought that I was quit of the spell cast by the Underground until I was lured back into it by my son. As a toddler, he'd preferred bus rides but he'd since switched allegiances to the Tube. And when I visited Zurich with him two years ago he fell in love with the city's trams. I made the mistake of catching the wrong tram with some friends and became a laughing stock in front of my son. When I occasionally use the Underground with him, he is very watchful that we don't catch a train in the wrong direction. It's an easy mistake to make, particularly when the line branches into two. People who fall asleep in the Tube often find that they have missed their station and ended up elsewhere.

I had walked past the London Transport Museum in Covent Garden many times but never ventured inside except to buy the odd postcard in its gift-shop. However, I was recently inspired by my son to visit it with him. He has memorised the kind of trivia about the Underground that you are expected to know by heart if you take part in a pub quiz. In fact, it was only after riding a new tube train with him, and he asked me to put my hand over a vent to check if it was cold air, that I realised the new carriages come with air conditioning. Before this, I'd only ever seen the industrial-size fans, which look more like aircraft propellers, sitting idle in a corner under a shaft in the Underground, and I yearned to see them in action. The only gusts of air you are hit by while standing on a station platform are propelled through the tunnel by the trains themselves. Their flat fronts seem deliberately designed for the purpose of circulating air below ground.

The London Underground is indeed a marvel of British engineering but its saviour at the beginning of the 20th Century was an American financier, Charles Tyson Yerkes, who set up a company in London that electrified and completed the Underground projects that had run into financial difficulties.

If all the world's a stage, then London's Underground is a microcosm of such a world. Doris Lessing had found it bizarre to see Indian women wearing cardigans over their saris in the Tube. But today you can sometimes see European woman dressed elegantly in saris, with a decorative *bindi* mark on their foreheads, their hair neatly tied back and parted in the middle. It is sights like these that make the experience of riding the London Underground so memorable.

The Curse of The Bishops Avenue

In 1995, after living in Harringay in North London for a year or so, I packed my bags and moved to South Hill Park near Hampstead Heath. I had arrived in London with nothing but a holdall bag but gradually acquired a few household things and needed a cab to move my belongings to the new accommodation. It was a room on the top floor of a large house on the edge of the Heath. The cabbie drove through Muswell Hill, then along a narrow road, passing a cinema in East Finchley (one of the oldest still functioning in Britain, I was later to learn), and next turned into an avenue with large splendid-looking houses on either side. Pointing out these mansions, the driver informed me that they belonged to very wealthy people and that the road was named The Bishops Avenue. He wore a blazer and a white shirt, rather too smartly dressed, I thought, for the old car he was driving. He was from Ghana, he said, and had been driving a cab in London for many years. He continued talking about the houses, explaining that most of them were empty and no one ever lived in them. It intrigued me to learn that such large London houses were left empty whereas small flats were occupied.

The driver pointed out the gates of a country-style house that he said was open to the public. There was a crenellated square logo denoting 'English Heritage' on its signboard, and I later learnt that this was a charitable organisation. The driver negotiated an awkward bend formed by a roadside pub and an old tollgate and drove up what looked like a country road before passing a pond. It was all downhill from there.

I was familiar with the South End of the Heath, having worked in a corner shop there when I settled in London the year before. I sometimes walked as far as Kenwood House and then back to South Hill Park while living in the neighbourhood, but never ventured beyond this stately home, which was bequeathed to the nation by an Anglo-Irish businessman.

I lived on the south side of the Heath for the next 12 years except for a year in East London and a year in Muswell Hill, and I'd quickly fallen in love with Hampstead Heath. I moved to East Finchley in 2007, which isn't too far from the Heath. This time I needed a van rather than a cab to move my belongings. I had bought a desk from a local shop called Second Time Around and made a few bookshelves myself, and the furniture filled the van up to the roof.

Aiming to cycle to work from home, I'd printed out a route map that took me along a busy road. However, I preferred to follow a map in my mind that pulled me back to ride along a road that cuts through the Heath. I passed Abbots Gardens on the way and then cycled down Deans Way to reach The Bishops Avenue. It was easy to guess from the names of these roads that all this land must have once belonged to the church. I met an Indian accountant in London who told me that he lived in Bishops Avenue, quickly adding that it was Bishops Avenue in Uxbridge, not 'The' Bishops Avenue on the north side of Hampstead Heath. When I told a co-worker in a bookshop where I briefly worked that I was living in Hampstead he commented with the deadpan expression of a comic actor that I must be living in a mansion, meaning a house in The Bishops Avenue.

I finished work at midnight as usual when I moved to the new neighbourhood and cycled uphill to reach the pond called Whitestone. Like the panting carriage-horses that in earlier years waded through this pond to cool off, it was always with a sigh of relief that I saw Jack Straw's Castle beside Whitestone pond on the crest of the hill. Its name had long baffled me because it has battlements made of wood rather than stone. Camden's Pirate Castle was at least made of bricks.

It was a straight ride through the Heath along Spaniards Road until I reached the old Spaniards Inn and waited for the oncoming vehicles with their blinding headlights to give me the right of way through the tollgate. You can still find an old cattle trough made of stone on one side of this road.

I would cruise downhill on my bike from there before turning left into The Bishops Avenue. I recall one of my first cycle-rides home. It was the middle of the night. The road was dimly lit and felt eerily quiet at this late hour. Dick Turpin, the legendary highwayman who lurked in the darkness in this area in the 18th century, came to mind. I felt anxious that if anyone were to rob me here, no one would come to my rescue even if I shouted at the top of my voice. As this ominous thought crossed my mind, I noticed a car driving slowly behind me as if its driver and his passenger accomplice were looking for a suitably dark place to rob me on this deserted road. I let the slow-moving car overtake me and watched it drive for a hundred yards before it made a U-turn. I became convinced that they'd made up their minds to rob me after ensuring there was no pedestrian around to bear witness to their crime. My heart beat faster. I looked away as the car approached and it was a great relief when it drove straight past me. I didn't look back until I reached a busy intersection with many cars and lorries reassuringly driving along the main road.

I have felt no fear since then in cycling down the Avenue at night although it appears to be a ghost road. Sometimes I see a lone resident walking her dog in the dead of night and if our eyes meet she nods her head in acknowledgement. At first I was surprised to witness this nocturnal civility in so desolate a part of London. One night I found a group of photographers, wielding cameras with extended lenses mounted on tripods, gathered outside a mansion in the Avenue as if re-enacting a *paparazzi* scene from Fellini's *La Dolce Vita*. I came to learn a few days later that a globe-trotting rock-star had taken residence in the house for a few days and the photographers stood ready outside the gates to take photos of him in case he popped out from his temporary home for a night-time excursion.

I felt sympathy for the photographers since it's a tough way of making a living, waiting indefinitely at a roadside throughout the night, hoping that some celebrity will go somewhere on a whim at the witching hour. I had thought it was bad for me to finish work at midnight until I saw these poor souls standing outside in the cold, their vigil only just begun.

It is a different scene during the day, though, in The Bishops Avenue. A lot of cars and vans are parked on both sides of the road, belonging to builders working on various sites. You can also see a few large coaches in an unmarked section of the road. The coach drivers park them there while waiting between jobs in town. Sometimes I spot a black or a white stretch limo parked outside a mansion. And occasionally big lorries and caravans belonging to a TV or film company are parked in an adjacent road since the empty mansions in the area are ideal for location shooting.

I have witnessed exactly the same scenes in the Avenue for 12 years since I started riding my bike through it five days a week. These include the trucks and cement mixers driving in and out, and the parked vans with adverts for services like landscape gardening and swimming pool maintenance. When I first moved to the south side of the Heath I saw big removal trucks so frequently that I marvelled at how often people moved from one neighbourhood to another in London. My parents moved into a new neighbourhood in Srinagar when I was a young man and I had found it rather alienating to move from a neighbourhood where I had friends to a new one where I had none. However, despite seeing building work going on at properties in The Bishops Avenue, I have never seen a parked removal truck hired by someone who is either moving in or moving out.

A few smaller houses in the middle of the Avenue seemed to be lived in. One afternoon I saw my GP outside one of these houses and she told me that she had been to see a patient in a care home there. I would never have guessed that there could be a care home among the derelict dwellings in the Avenue. You only find rude notices such as 'KEEP OUT' tied to the fences of houses around here. Many of these notice boards have a picture of a threatening-looking dog attached to them but you just know there is no dog inside any empty house here and the picture is just there to discourage trespassers.

I have noticed some of the houses being redecorated a few times during the last decade but no one ever living in them, thus confirming what the cab driver had told me years ago. When a house in The Bishops Avenue changes hands, it is remodelled according to the taste of its new owner, who never chooses to live in it before putting it back on the market. An old Cape Dutch-style home was recently refurbished and featured on the homepage of an internet-browser. The reporter asked whether a relatively small house in the Avenue justified its enormous price tag. But this was more by way of an advertising ploy than a genuine insight into property prices in London. A few trees were planted in its manicured garden before a FOR SALE signboard was erected. I was curious whether they'd be able to sell the house after all the hype until I saw security warning notices appear all over its fence a few months later.

I usually get to know more about the goings-on in my local area from mini-cab drivers than from newspapers. I saw a house badly damaged by fire when, as usual, I rode my bike through the Avenue one afternoon six years ago. A few months later I saw scaffolding going up and builders working on the repair of its roof. It wasn't until a year later, when I was sitting in the back of a cab, that the driver pointed out the house and told me that an elderly man living in the house had stabbed his wife to death before setting the house on fire.

I hire a cab from work only when I have a flat tyre and have to carry my bike home to repair it. A cab driver who gave me a ride home along with my bike one night informed me when he drove past one of the biggest mansions in the Avenue that he sometimes picked up a lady he called 'Madam Nur' from that house. I wasn't sure, though, if he knew that the house belonged to the president of Kazakhstan.

The Bishops Avenue is empty at weekends except for the cars parked at its top end by people who visit the Heath for a walk. I went to work at the break of dawn for a few months one year and encountered a jogger walking in the opposite direction at the exact same spot each day, so regularly that I could have set accurate time on my watch by his appearance. I had met him in the hotel where I work and knew he lived four miles to the north of the Heath. So he must have got up extremely early each morning to reach the Heath before daybreak.

I look out for potholes when I cycle down The Bishops Avenue in the dark because the road is strewn with rubbish at night. The new buildings have tidy pavements whereas the derelict houses have unkempt front lawns. The cypresses belonging to one of these houses have grown so tall that they effectively conceal the three-storied house behind them. An estate agent has put up a large FOR SALE signboard outside, advertising it as 'a magnificent freehold'. However the state of disrepair of the house belies the word 'magnificent'.

The large houses in the Avenue wouldn't look particularly outlandish in another city but most of the people of London live in very small flats or houses and when you see a house for sale which boasts an area of 24,000 square feet you realize it is 40 times bigger than an average one-bedroom flat in London. Aerial pictures show lots of land, including arboretums, that lies hidden from the gaze of the ramblers who sometimes drift into the Avenue after walking on the Heath. On sunny days I also find that people, having parked their cars in the Avenue with a view to walking on the Heath, take photographs of the mansions through their wrought-iron gates.

London is a densely populated city and teaches its residents how to live in close proximity to our neighbours. But the wealthy owners of The Bishops Avenue houses, which they hardly ever occupy, would rather have an empty house next door than be seen by a neighbour. You could easily hide in a house there if you were on the run.

It is an uphill ride for me from home to work until I get to the Spaniards Inn. The Bishops Avenue is a long road but it is intersected by only one other, and so you sometimes find a driver in a sports car driving through it at great speed. There is a slight bend in the road and when I reach it and see a traffic light in the distance, it gives me courage to peddle on and catch the splintered light of the sun through the high trees. From the Spaniards Inn on the way back to my home is an easy ride during the night. I occasionally see a few teenage girls waiting outside the home of another rock-star in hope of catching a glimpse of him. I once saw two girls leaving red roses outside his gate, which is painted black, and one of them threw a rose over it. I caught sight of their heartthrob one night when he sneaked out of his home in running gear and froze like a stunned antelope when I crossed his path on my bike.

There are actually only sixty-odd houses in the entire length of the Avenue. Some of these are in good condition whereas others are boarded up. The routine of buying, doing up, and then selling a house in Bishops Avenue without ever living in it is seemingly endless. The new owners do up their houses before putting them back on the market, keeping many builders and one particular estate agent in regular business. I sometimes pass the office of this estate agent when I cycle to work by an alternative route. I cut through Hampstead

Garden Suburb, which is dominated by the spire of St Jude's Church. The road is flanked by Turner Close on one side and Ruskin Close on the other. When I cycled past it for the first time, it struck me as rather remarkable that a painter and an art critic have occupied opposite sides of the same road in peaceful co-existence for decades. The estate agent's office is located at the corner of a vast cemetery. The landlords of London don't usually let their shops to undertakers, so the owners of mansions in the Avenue are likely to be spooked by the sight when they pop into their agent's office.

A certain house in the Avenue has one of those pictures of a menacing guard dog on a signboard nailed to its gate with the message 'I can make it to the gate in 3 secs'. Its windows are fitted with metal shutters. When I ride home late at night, I find the front and back lawn of this house illuminated by bright floodlights. It is one of the few houses in this road that is actually occupied and there is always a security patrol car parked beside it. In fact, when cycling through The Bishops Avenue at night, I see security cars cruising more often than any other kind of vehicle.

One night, I saw a party in full swing in one of the mansions. A tree in its garden had a long garland made of marigolds hung on one of its branches, the way you tie a garland around the neck of a statue of a Hindu goddess. At first I thought they were real marigolds. But since they didn't wither over a period of several weeks, I realized they were made of plastic.

On another occasion I bumped into someone who'd worked with me in a bookshop but was now a personal trainer. He was accompanying a client on his walk along The Bishops Avenue. He had been hired by a wealthy Indian family living in the area to get their son, who was feeling a bit low, into a regular exercise regime.

A Black Cab driver once hooted behind me as I was cycling home through the Avenue during a wintry snowfall. Since the road was empty, I felt flustered and stopped to see why he was hooting. The driver turned out to be an acquaintance of mine, offering to give me – and my bike – a lift home.

I do find it rather strange how the absentee owners of the mansions in the Avenue set about their business. When a property changes hands, I usually see men in suits, who must have accreditations from the Royal Institute of Surveyors, arrive at the site wearing yellow hard hats and carrying clipboards. The architects hired by the new owners prepare drawings for the changes in their property to be carried out, which are usually very extensive. The diggers and excavators arrive at the site soon after and the remodelling takes several months. But even when the building is ready, it remains empty for many more months until the usual notices are fastened to its fence announcing that the building is monitored by remote surveillance.

*

A Greek businessman was shot dead in his home in The Bishops Avenue a few decades ago and legend has it that the bullet is still embedded in a wall of the house. When I lived in South Hill Park, I passed a pub on the way, outside which Ruth Ellis, the last woman to be hanged in Britain, had shot dead her lover in 1955, and I always took a moment to look at two dark spots believed to be the bullet holes in its exterior wall. The blonde landlady of the pub would come into the corner shop where I worked to get change. She was always cheerful and chatty.

The shopkeeper I worked for was annoyed that one of her customers, an estate agent, owed her a few pounds for his daily snack. She left a message with me asking him to pay his debt. When I gave him the message he merely smiled and told me to let her know that he hadn't yet left the country. This annoyed the shopkeeper even more and she instructed me not to sell him anything on credit. Many years later, I saw the same agent walking in The Bishops Avenue and asked him if he was there to show a house to a prospective buyer. He chuckled and replied that he wished it were true so he could take early retirement.

I wasn't sure who the men in pinstripe suits and neat haircuts were when I saw them for the first time in the corner shop, buying newspapers and snacks at lunchtime, not until I gathered that they were estate agents and therefore had to dress formally to sell an expensive flat or house in the neighbourhood. I have known only one such broker in Srinagar.

He had become the talk of the town for wearing a sharp suit and carrying a portfolio wherever he went. He was distrusted more than other brokers and could pull the wool over a client's eyes because he was so articulate. One day I saw him sitting in my father's shop. Since my father couldn't read or write, he was extremely wary lest the agent persuade him to buy some disputed property. At first it puzzled me why these genial, elegantly dressed gents were also thought of as untrustworthy by Londoners. When I was searching for a home, I liked to make enquiries with an elderly estate agent whose face would become reddened by alcohol in the afternoon. But he seemed to me to be both reticent and compassionate compared to his slick younger colleagues who spoke so persuasively about the merits of the properties they advertised.

I think you have to be pretty audacious to describe a dilapidated house in The Bishop Avenue as 'magnificent' when a client can see plants growing in its cracks and the brickwork turned green by the growth of moss on its exterior. What a breathless spiel an agent must deliver in order to make a wealthy person part with a large quantity of cash by way of acquiring a house in this very expensive part of London.

*

When I moved to East Finchley, I drifted into an Adult Education college housed in a modern building at one end of The Bishops Avenue and came across an acquaintance from my old neighbourhood at the reception desk. I had found him interesting to chat to whenever he came into the corner shop and was impressed by his knowledge of cinema and literature. He had grown up in a bilingual home. He told me that his mother was Spanish and his father was English and that kids at his school sometimes made fun of him for the way he pronounced certain words. When I asked him about the institute he was currently working for he said that it was facing a funding crisis and they might have to move out soon. I was familiar with this institute, having attended a course there in Hampstead Garden Suburb, and was sorry to hear about its financial difficulties. It was surprising, though, to find an Adult Education college at one end of the Avenue, an old age home towards the middle and many empty houses in between.

*

During the night, I usually ride my bike through the Avenue without looking left or right as if I am wearing blinkers, and I don't stop anywhere along this road because I know that I am being watched remotely through the cameras mounted on the gates and walls of the houses. I wouldn't like anyone to feel unduly alarmed and therefore alert the security patrol personnel sitting in a car in a side road. I had read an excerpt from Orwell's *Nineteen Eighty-Four* in a newspaper in Kashmir in 1984 and considered that the bleak future he predicted, when two-way telescreens would be ubiquitous and privacy no longer existed, was a very distant prospect. When I saw a plaque above the door of a house in Hampstead where George Orwell lived, I took a picture and sent it to my mother. She had never heard of Orwell but framed the picture and displayed it in her glass cabinet.

Someone in Hampstead mentioned to me that Orwell had worked in a bookshop not far from his home but it doesn't exist any more. When I moved to Hampstead I sat in the restaurant of a Highgate youth hostel and read Orwell's *Down and Out in Paris and London*. An Australian woman staying at the hostel remarked that it was a grim title for a book. However, Orwell's observations about London still rang very true to me nine decades after he had written them. I once met a speechwriter in the corner shop who told me that he always followed Orwell's advice and wrote his speeches in simple English. But an English tutor I knew who taught foreign students in London expressed his disdain by saying that he would never read a book by "some socialist like George Orwell".

A large signboard in The Bishop's Avenue advertises several houses for sale as a 'Collection'. I'd heard of a collection of watches or cars but never a collection of derelict houses. Perhaps the houses are all owned by a single wealthy family because I have never seen any of them inhabited at any time during the last 12 years. The lights aren't on during the night and it's obvious that nobody is living in what is fancifully referred to as a Collection. The notices on their fences warn onlookers that trespassers will be prosecuted. A new block of flats in the Avenue, however, features a fountain in its courtyard. I see water gushing from it whenever I ride past its gates during the night and it seems like an oasis in a wasteland because the lights of the flats are actually on.

A T-junction connects the Avenue with Hampstead Village on one side and Highgate Village on the other. In the beginning, when I stopped at the traffic lights there, it felt as if I had reached the point in Proust's novel at which one way leads to Combray and the other to Guermantes, so hard did I find it to decide on my cycling route to Central London. But after a few months of being pulled in both directions, I chose the Hampstead route. On my way back, I found West Hill leading to Highgate steeper than Fitzjohn's Avenue, which leads to Hampstead High Street. I got off my bike before reaching the top of the hill when I cycled via Highgate, passing a house which belongs to the Russian embassy and is fitted with security cameras all around it, whereas the Dutch House in Fitzjohn's Avenue exudes into the night air a sweet fragrance from some hidden flowering trees during the summer.

A house at the top of West Hill was used for the filming of a talent show for a TV channel and I found the vehicles for the crew parked in front of it during that time. When the property changed hands, the pavement was closed for some time for repairs to its tall perimeter wall, and it became hazardous to walk with my bike on the road, which I was obliged to do because cycling up this steep hill is very strenuous. One day I came across an old friend resting on a bench halfway up West Hill, his bike reclining against a wall. It was the author John Hands. I recognised him from a long way off because he sported a distinctive white Whitmanesque beard. I was pleased to see him again after such a long time – he used to chat with me at the counter when he came into the corner shop. And here he was, still cycling in his eighties.

I enjoyed my long walks and picnics on the Heath when I moved to South Hill Park and it seemed to me to be the only advantage of living in Hampstead. I met someone who ran a business from premises in the neighbourhood after my first book came out and he corrected a statement I'd made by saying that it isn't the residents of Hampstead who are snobbish but the lordly people living in the even more expensive area of St John's Wood. That made me smile.

Sometimes I took a woven Kilim rug and a book to read under a tree on the Heath and at other times I invited people with whom I'd become friends in the West End for a picnic on the Heath. I still like taking anyone coming to see me at home for a walk on the Heath.

I wasn't even familiar with the word 'Heath' when I moved to Hampstead and couldn't precisely describe its topography to my friends. It was a long time before I realized that Heathrow must have been a heath once, a hamlet with a row of houses at its edge. Although I'd heard about the oaks and beeches in the woodlands of Hampstead Heath, I wasn't able to identify those trees. I was also unaware that London had given its name to a type of plane tree that you find in abundance in the town. I've since heard that New York has many London plane trees. In fact, this tree seems to me like a smaller version of the giant Chinar tree that grows in Kashmir.

I haven't encountered any antlered deer crossing the road that runs through the Heath in the last twelve years. However, you can see brown rabbits running through the grass in the spring, and it is a joy to see azaleas and rhododendrons in full bloom in the grounds of Kenwood House. Inspired by the ode by John Keats, I longed to find a nightingale. But a birdwatcher I met told me that he hadn't seen a nightingale on the Heath for decades.

I drifted to the other side of Parliament Hill one afternoon and found an art installation on the grass called The Writer, in the form of a giant table and chair. It was by an Italian sculptor. He described it as 'a monument to the loneliness of writing' since writers are traditionally bound to their desks. For my part, I have always held Hampstead Heath in great sanctity because it affords me freedom from the confines of my room, enabling me to walk through a vast expanse of parkland at my very doorstep. And when I ride my bike through the Heath along Spaniards Road, my mind wanders in a different realm where ideas occur about what to write on a blank screen the next day.

King's Cross Resurrected

On the first day of March 2011, I received a phone call from a reporter from a local paper to let me know that the St Pancras Hotel in King's Cross was soon going to open its doors to the public. He asked me if I could write a feature on this iconic building for his newspaper. I was in Mumbai when I picked up the call, travelling in an auto-rickshaw outside the Victoria Terminus now known as CST – a building that bears an uncanny resemblance to the one housing the St Pancras Hotel except that it is made of sandstone whereas the one in London is made of bricks. I'd like to have been back in London to tour the building that had intrigued me for years whenever I visited the British Library. I didn't know the reason for it being left empty. The clock tower of this Victorian Gothic building actually dwarfed that of the recently built Library.

It was Robert the Concierge, who told me that the landmark building at King's Cross was going to be restored and would open as a hotel. It could take years of painstaking work, he said, to bring this building, which was originally built as the Midland Grand Hotel during the golden age of the railways, back to its former glory. The name King's Cross evoked images of a grungy part of London before the regeneration of the area started 20 years ago. An acquaintance of mine from Punjab liked to drop the possessive and call it King Cross. When I cycled through the back roads of the area for the first time and saw the rusty giant gasholders, it was like drifting into an industrial wasteland. I shunned the area until the British Library moved to Euston Road from Great Russell Street in 1997 and I subsequently often visited one of its reading rooms.

The first high-speed train arrived in 2007 when the Eurostar moved from Waterloo to St Pancras station. In 2008 the Guardian newspaper moved its offices from 119 Farringdon Road to a swanky new glass building in the area, and King's Cross became the biggest transport hub in Europe. I often went to St Pancras station to meet a friend for coffee who commuted on a high-speed train to Kent, and I once attended the wedding of another friend in the Town Hall in Judd Street. I visited the Town Hall again when my son was born to get a birth certificate for him and sat with a registrar of births, a good-natured Bengali lady, in an office overlooking the St Pancras Hotel.

When Robert the Concierge broke the news of the new hotel to be opened in King's Cross, the landmark building in Midland Road looked somewhat spooky. Whenever I took a Eurostar train from St Pancras during the next few years, I found a lot of construction work going on around the building while it was being restored, to open more than a century and a half after it was purpose-built as a hotel. I passed by the hotel many times after it opened, noticing a doorman wearing a bowler hat and waistcoat standing outside, but couldn't think of an excuse to go inside. I found myself closer to the hotel while standing in the Arcade of St Pancras station and caught sight of the enormous bronze statue known as The Lovers, plus a gilded Dent clock. Sometimes someone would break into a tune on the piano in the Arcade, causing brisk walkers to come to a halt during their daily commute.

I had wondered what the St Pancras Hotel looked like from the inside until in 2016 I happened to meet its manager by chance in our hotel and she suggested that I pay a visit. I cycled through Camden as usual to get there and saw the futuristic new building of the Francis Crick Institute standing tall in Midland Road before I reached the British Library, which was hosting a 'Shakespeare in Ten Acts' exhibition until September that year.

I locked my bike in a rack outside the British Library and walked up the driveway of the St Pancras Hotel to be welcomed by the bowler-hatted doorman. A white Rolls Royce parked in the forecourt displayed 'WISHS X' as its number-plate. But walking into the lobby of the hotel felt like travelling back in time. Behind the Reception Desk there is a hall that has been turned into a bar and restaurant, though still called the Booking Office. The manager had very kindly asked one of her staff to show me around. She took me through the Booking Office and then through a door at the back that opened directly into St Pancras station where a Eurostar train was standing at the platform. It was surreal to see a high-speed train – a marvel of modern engineering – in front of the St Pancras Hotel, which was built when trains were powered by steam engines. My host also showed me the ladies smoking room which must have caused a scandal during Victorian times when you couldn't even mention the word 'trousers' in front of a lady.

George Gilbert Scott, son of a clergyman, had designed the original Midland Grand Hotel – now the St Pancras Hotel – like a cathedral. Images of the seven Christian virtues are painted on the wall at the top of its spiralling staircase, and when you lower your gaze from the landing it induces vertigo. I was shown a room named after Queen Victoria. It has a very high ceiling and one of the walls is painted in emerald green. It's a most spacious room, as befits a larger-than-life Queen.

The opening of the St Pancras Hotel has played a part in the rebirth of King's Cross. I can imagine guests arriving in the horse-drawn vehicles known as hansom cabs when it was called the Midland Grand Hotel. Today travellers can enjoy afternoon tea in the Hansom Lounge of the St Pancras Hotel. It has two miniature statues of The Lovers, otherwise identical to the one in St Pancras station, on display in a Perspex box in the hotel lobby.

*

King's Cross appeared to be a dingy kind of area when I walked out of its Underground station for the first time. In fact, the plans for its regeneration were drawn up before I moved to London. However, it took many more years for the work to begin on the various projects entailed. I sometimes went to meet a friend from Kashmir who worked at a travel agency at the nearby Euston station. The walk from King's Cross to Euston station was a nightmarish experience during which you bumped into habitual drug-users, some of whom asked you for a pound.

One day a Bengali woman came into the shop in which I then worked in Hampstead and mentioned that she had seen me a few days before in King's Cross. I became anxious in case she asked me what I was doing in such a rough neighbourhood. I had been robbed in one of the backstreets near King's Cross a few months before. I'd shouted for help and, to my surprise, a policeman instantly appeared, like a genie. I was new in the country and therefore fearful of giving him my name and address.

I wasn't sure which monarch had lent his name to King's Cross until recently, when my son wanted to dress up as a king on a costume day at his school to show his liking for any train station in London. He chose King's Cross. It was actually King George IV whose statue once stood at the crossroads at King's Cross, thereby giving the area its name. But since we were unable to find a costume in the correct period, my son had to dress up as King Arthur instead.

I had heard much about an arch at Euston that had also been demolished, like the King's statue, and during my first few years in London I mistook a church near the station that has Doric columns and caryatids in its façade for the missing arch.

Euston Road offers an ever-changing prospect of the London cityscape. It has a gothic building and an old train station at one end, shiny glass buildings rising in the middle, and a crescent at the other end serving as a landmark of Regency London. I always like to cycle along the Outer Circle of Regent's Park on my way home from Central London.

A triangular cast-iron milestone in my neighbourhood has got '5 miles to Regent's Park from Parish of Finchley' embossed on it. A section of this road between Ballards Lane and Finchley Road is named Regent's Park Road. There are two roads in London that have been given this name – the other one being the road that connects Haverstock Hill with Regent's Park. Finchley Road runs along a winding path until it reaches Swiss Cottage and then follows a dangerous double bend towards St John's Wood.

The unbroken rows of houses and shops in Finchley Road give way to detached homes in Avenue Road and some of these homes are used as diplomatic residences. This elegant road joins the Outer Circle of Regent's Park at the other end after crossing an arched bridge over the Grand Union Canal that once connected London with Birmingham. For many years, I couldn't figure out how the boats passed through the lock in Camden on this canal until I took a boat cruise in Strasbourg in France and saw with my own eyes the opening and closing of the locks on a similar canal.

When I cycle to Central London via Regent's Park, I usually find a lot of keen runners and cyclists in Spandex shorts doing laps around the Outer Circle of the park. Outside Winfield House, the residence of the American ambassador to the UK, a solitary policeman stands guard, holding an automatic weapon close to his chest with one finger on the trigger. Sometimes when I pass him on my bike, I feel like greeting him, but then it occurs to me that it could frighten him into pulling the trigger. One early evening a few years ago, I found the road blocked and a policewoman advised me to take an alternative route to the other side of the park. I didn't know the reason for the closure until I saw men in tuxedos getting out of chauffeured cars with women in cocktail dresses on their arms, heading towards Winfield House, and I realised that the American ambassador was hosting a party at his home.

The minaret and copper dome of the London Central Mosque overlooks Winfield House. On Fridays, one finds cars belonging to various embassies in London waiting outside for plenipotentiaries who come here to attend midday prayers. So it looks as if East and West can coexist side by side on a patch of Regent's Park.

A white stucco building with cupolas houses the London Business School. It was designed by John Nash, like other terraced houses and villas along the periphery of

Regent's Park. No, not John Nash the twentieth century mathematician but the nineteenth century architect who acted as the master planner of Regent's Park. Sometimes I see a group of international students from the nearby University of Westminster being led by a guide on a tour of Regency London represented by the houses around this park. My guidebook says that we have Henry VIII to thank for Regent's Park, which he confiscated from the Church to use as hunting grounds, and my London compendium states that King Henry's Road, to the north of Primrose Hill, takes its name from Henry VI, who gave land to Eton College. However, it was during Queen Victoria's reign that Primrose Hill was obtained for the Crown in exchange for the land that Eton College had received.

Primrose Hill is today considered to be part of Regent's Park and offers a panoramic view of London. When visitors gather on top of the hill, they find an inscription in York stone which reads 'I have conversed with the spiritual Sun. I saw him on Primrose Hill.' This is attributed to William Blake, who worked as an engraver and remained obscure as a poet in his lifetime.

London Zoo lies at the foot of this hill. There is a lion's den and butterfly paradise inside the zoo. Before leaving the zoo, visitors are allowed to trade places for a moment and stand behind a wire fence to have a picture taken in front of a sign above stating 'The most destructive animal in the world'.

Regent's Park is tucked away from the hordes that

descend on Hyde Park during the summer months because the Outer Circle of the park isn't used as a bus route, unlike Park Lane. I hear there are plans to close the gates of the park to traffic during peak hours so that cyclists can use it as a highway to travel in and out of London. Two new events have been initiated in Regent's Park during the last decade. The Frieze Art Fair and Taste of London bring an affluent crowd to the park. The former is a gathering of gallery owners showcasing and selling their wares, and the latter features restaurateurs who offer a sample tasting of their food for a fee.

Queen Mary's rose garden in the Inner Circle of Regent's Park is usually in bloom in May every year. Also located in the sanctum of the park is the long-established Open Air Theatre presenting plays from May to September. In 2016 it presented *Henry V* by Shakespeare with the title role played by an actress, a nice reversal of the Elizabethan practice of female roles being played by boys. Such cross-gender Shakespeare productions, some with all-female casts, have become increasingly popular.

I took a leisurely walk through the centre of the park one summer's afternoon and when I reached a secluded garden I came across a group of women lying bare-bosomed in the sun. It was like a re-enactment of the scene in Manet's *Le Déjeuner sur l'herbe*, in which two men in full attire are sitting in the company of two naked beauties. Like those men, I looked away and walked hurriedly towards the gates of the park.

Whenever I cycle past Great Portland Street station in Marylebone Road I am reminded of a similar-looking building in Delhi, designed by Edwin Lutyens and known as Gole Market, which constitutes a traffic roundabout. Marylebone Road becomes Euston Road and, after traversing an underpass, an imposing building housing the Wellcome Collection is followed by a big brick building that is owned by Quakers, endearingly referred to by them as Friends House. When I first moved to Hampstead, I was intrigued to find a small Friends House in Heath Street, where a Buddhist monk gave talks on meditation once a week. One evening I walked in and bumped into an American whom I'd served in the corner shop. He didn't look well. But then he never did – perhaps that was the reason why he was there.

The British Library's move to Euston Road in 1997 has played a big part in the regeneration of King's Cross. I was bewitched to see its circular reading room inside the British Museum. Karl Marx was a habitué of this reading room. He was thrown out of many European countries before finding refuge in Britain. And he was later thrown out of his home in Soho by his landlady.

The British Library was a kind of spiritual home for me when I moved to Hampstead. It was only a short hop away on my bike and was a good place for me to meet acquaintances from Kashmir visiting London for a few days. On my days off from work I sat either in the foyer or in one of its reading rooms. I also liked to browse in its bookshop.

The British Library shop is unlike any other bookshop. On the way to the Library, you go through the bronze gates into a piazza, pass an amphitheatre and the colossus of Eduardo Paolozzi's 'Newton' – and you are transported to another world. The bookshop is located close by the entrance. In the corner is a statue of Shakespeare in a reflective posture, sculpted by Louis-François Roubiliac. On the opposite wall hangs a tapestry based on Kitaj's enigmatic drawing *If Not, Not*, depicting a man wearing a jacket and tie lying on the ground close to the contours of a female breast. A gently flowing fountain is emblematic of the serenity inside the library.

At the counter of the British Library Bookshop one often finds white-bearded scholars paying for books. The coffee shops and restaurant are where fellow-writers and researchers meet after using various reading rooms. The main coffee shop is hidden behind a glass tower lined with leather-bound volumes that once belonged to George III. The coffee shop in the piazza is known as 'The Last Word'. And it's customary for many readers and visitors to browse in the bookshop before leaving the library.

In 2007 I observed that one of the walls was allocated to 'Books about Books'. It was arguably the biggest selection of books on bibliography stocked by a bookshop in the UK, if not in the world. One could find such wide-ranging titles as *The Art of the Book* and The Story of Writing among the volumes on these shelves. The adjoining wall had books on Cartography, Business, Natural History and Science. The other side displayed sections on Reference, Classics, Poetry and Plays, while Fiction, Biography and History were arranged on the lower shelves. And the shop stocked fine editions of Classics.

The British Library publishes a number of titles every year relating to the exhibitions taking place there and on other subjects. These titles are always much sought after by those who come to see the exhibitions, one of which, London: A Life in Maps, brought thousands of visitors to the Library. It was during this exhibition that the shop was extended into the foyer of the library. The shop had a permanent section of books on London. Besides books, the BL shop sold a number of gift items such as calligraphy sets, LED book-lights, posters, bookmarks and pencils bearing the name of the library. It is almost a fetish for some writers to use the pencils that are sold only in this shop.

Some of the big publishers mistakenly regard the British Library Bookshop as a heritage shop and don't send their sales reps there. Others working in the publishing industry don't seem to be aware of the shop's existence. Perhaps they haven't visited the British Library since it moved to Euston Road. A few of them probably still like to associate it with 'Bloomsbury'. In fact, the British Library Bookshop is a great supporter of small publishers and sells hundreds of copies of titles often shunned by the chains.

Taking the needs of their customers into consideration, the BL shop started selling the LRB, TLS and other magazines. Money made by the bookshop generally goes back into the library for the benefit of its readers.

*

My bike ride to the British Library from Hampstead took me through Camden Town and then through various backstreets, past the gilded wrought-iron gates of an old church; and when I saw the wooden frames outside a workshop that made cabinets for radiators, I knew I'd shortly be at home again in the BL. However, the cement mixers that brought concrete for the new developments around King's Cross posed a mortal threat to cyclists. I was saddened to see the picture in a local newspaper of a fellow-cyclist from my neighbourhood after she was crushed to death by a truck near King's Cross. I had seen her many times in the stationers where I worked in Hampstead and she usually wore a helmet and a high visibility vest. But it was only after reading the report of her death in a newspaper that I came to know that she was the daughter of the typewriter manufacturer, Adriano Olivetti. I typed my first book on an Olivetti Studio 44 and this compact manual typewriter is the most valuable item I possess in London.

King's Cross station was redeveloped for the London Olympics as a quick link to the Olympic Park in Stratford. High-speed trains were run between King's Cross and Stratford to carry spectators plus the members of the International Olympic Committee who stayed at the St Pancras Hotel. The gigantic Olympic rings, made of steel, were hung above the platforms at St Pancras station in front of the Dent Clock, which was originally made for the Great Exhibition of 1851. The train station at Queen Elizabeth Olympic Park was ostentatiously named 'Stratford International' even though it connected to Eurostar only through an interchange.

I well remember the euphoria when, on the 6th of July 2007, London won the bid to host the Games of the XXX Olympiad. An elderly lady in Hampstead told me how proud she had felt watching the jubilant crowd at Trafalgar Square celebrating the news about her home city winning the bid to host the Games for the third time.

But sadly, the next day, bombs went off at various London Underground stations including King's Cross, and a bus was blown up near Euston. I had arranged to meet an acquaintance from Kashmir that day in the British Library. I had planned to go there by bike as usual but my guest was going to take a bus and I feared for her safety. When I finally met her a week later she said that she believed London was one of the safest cities in the world and never imagined that overnight it could become more dangerous than Srinagar.

Londoners spent the next few years in anticipation of hosting this big event as men and machinery moved into East London to build the venues for the Games. As a child, I had gone to a cinema in Kashmir to watch a film about the Moscow Olympics of 1980 and was bedazzled to see it on a big screen in full colour as I was accustomed to seeing only grainy television pictures in black and white. When the Asian Games were held in New Delhi in 1982, I was transfixed by the games broadcast on television and was very keen to travel to Delhi afterwards to train as a sportsman.

We expected 2012 to be our busiest year at the hotel

where I work and a lot of hotels in London were getting ready to host the members of Olympic committees of various countries. Because security in the city hosting the Games is always a big concern, hotels in London trained their staff to deal with any eventuality.

Our hotel happened to be on the path of the Olympic torch relay and therefore provided a night's accommodation for a big entourage. However, I didn't get a chance to hold the Olympic torch in my hands as it happened to be my day off at work. We were given the logos of the London Olympics to wear as badges on the lapels of our uniform jackets. One of the logos had the Union Jack printed on it and another was plain white. I chose to wear the plain one at the panel discussion event in which I was invited to take part at the University of Geneva before the Games. My host was curious why I was wearing this badge and what it signified. When I met her before the event she asked me what book I was currently reading and I had to confess it was *Ghost Milk: Calling Time on the Grand Project* by Iain Sinclair, about the questionable legacy of the London Olympics.

As a matter of fact, I was ready to pack my bags and move back to Srinagar for good before the London Olympics. In an unsigned letter of refusal, the British Embassy in New Delhi had declined my wife's application for a Spouse Visa to visit London. I had no wish to go through the rigmarole of an appeal process and wait indefinitely for the arrival of my wife in London. So I couldn't help but make a fuss about it with the Home Office. It paid off. Just a couple of weeks before the start of the Games I received an unexpected email from the British High Commission in Delhi informing me that they had overturned their earlier decision and decided to grant a visa to my wife.

I booked my ticket to Delhi earlier than originally intended in order to accompany my wife, who had travelled from Kashmir to collect her visa from the British High Commission in the diplomatic enclave of Chanakyapuri. Heathrow airport felt welcoming, with flowers planted outside Terminal 5. How I'd yearned to live in a city that hosted the Olympics when I saw the highlights of the Moscow Games as I child in a cinema in Srinagar. I have watched the Games on television with great interest ever since the XXII Moscow Olympiad.

I sat with the filmmaker Marc Isaacs in the coffee shop of a hotel a few months before the Olympics. A colleague of mine asked him the reason for making his current documentary about a Roman road in London at a time when the city was hosting a world event and he quipped that the entire world was already here and one needs a fresh outlook and not a big event to see it.

Transport had remained an area of concern when the IOC awarded the hosting of the XXX Olympiad to London. The Underground was already overcrowded and during the Games it was bound to set a new record for the number of journeys made in a single day. No wonder some Londoners favoured the bid of a rival city for the hosting of the Olympics.

London always seems to be ready for the hosting of a big event like the Golden or Sapphire Jubilee of a reigning Monarch or an international convention that's attended by thousands of delegates. It had surprised me to learn when I started to work in a hotel that a flower show or an air show can fill hundreds of big London hotels at a time.

The involvement of volunteers and sponsors made the Olympics in London seem effortless. I saw a fleet of BMW cars ferrying officials from various hotels in London to the Olympic park and the volunteer stewards assisting their smooth passage looked quite content to wear the uniform supplied by the main sponsor of the Games. Would-be spectators were pleased to get their hands on tickets for any event through a lottery draw. As a keen cyclist, I was delighted that a velodrome had turned into a 'gold factory' (as they nicknamed it) for Team GB. Cycling in London became fashionable and I saw a lot more men and women in Lycra hitting the saddle after the Games.

I saw the Olympic Park for the first time from above when I crossed the Thames in a newly built cable car. It was funded by an airline that had given its name to this new addition to Transport for London just before the start of the Games. Many years before, I had crossed the Thames by foot through an underground tunnel at the bend of the river near Greenwich. I walked into a big shopping centre at Stratford East to see the Olympic Park from a viewing platform on its upper level. On my way back to the Underground station, I caught a glimpse of a large chorus of men and women singing and dancing in rehearsal for the opening ceremony of the Games.

I wasn't sure any more if I wanted to live in London in the foreseeable future. Not because London is hard work for its residents but because my pleading with the Home Office to issue a Spouse Visa for my wife had left a bad taste in my mouth. I had actually been on the point of leaving my adopted city of 18 years when the visa problem was suddenly resolved.

I recently revisited the British Library after a gap of many years. It has become a lot busier than it was in the days when I frequented it a decade and a half ago. King's Cross has attracted many tech companies and the area has become trendy after the regeneration effort. It is a far cry from the King's Cross of ill repute in the mid-1990s when I came to London. For instance, it used to have only nightclubs whereas now it has theatres. A new one has opened just behind King's Cross station which staged *The Railway Children*, based on E Nesbit's book, in its opening season.

When I used to meet a friend at St Pancras station, I saw builders restoring the German Gymnasium building outside it and wondered if it was going to be a gym. Then one day a restaurant opened there to lure in new office workers living in the area. The Arcade inside St Pancras station seems more crowded compared to the days when I sat inside a coffee shop there with a book and watched the world go by.

Every half an hour I would see a crew of Eurostar personnel walking past in their crisp uniforms, with yellow and blue scarves tied around their necks. They looked more like an airline crew than railway staff.

A man from the Indian subcontinent who had dyed his greying beard came now and again into the coffee shop I frequented. He was always accompanied by a European woman who was much younger than he was. She looked at him affectionately when they sat at a corner table and he seemed a bit embarrassed by it. Perhaps they worked in an office together and had embarked on a surreptitious relationship. It is always places of transience like railway stations – or hotels – that can offer you an insight into other people's secret worlds.

Vaisakhi Mela in Southall

A few years after I came to London, a friend drove me to Southall to have lunch at his uncle's. I had heard the name of this town in Middlesex even before I had heard of Camden Town in London. However, Southall appeared to be a much more distant place since it didn't have (and still hasn't) an Underground station. To reach Southall, I had to take the Underground to Ealing Broadway and then a bus from there.

The traffic came to a standstill before we reached Southall Broadway. I got out of the car to find out what had caused the jam and asked a group of children playing by the roadside. One of them said it was the Muslims' Christmas that day which is why so many people were heading to Southall. It happened in mid-April – a time for the celebration by Sikhs of the festival of Vaisakhi. The child had mistaken long-bearded Sikh men for Muslims, which made me smile. I knew a white-bearded Sikh man looks a bit like Father Christmas to children in the UK but was surprised that children would confuse Sikhs with Muslims.

Vaisakhi is the New Year in the Sikh calendar. It is also celebrated as a harvest festival in Punjab where two crops are grown in a year. The occasion is called Baisakhi in Kashmir and celebrated as a spring festival – a time for the sowing of crops to be reaped in autumn. It also marks the end of the cold season in Kashmir when people usually shed a layer of winter clothes and the gates of public gardens are thrown open. A Hindu festival in August marked the end of the hot spell of summer for my Muslim grandmother.

The association of Southall with Punjab goes back 60 years, when Punjabi men began to settle in the area. The town, which lies outside London, still has the look of an industrial area. The men from Punjab worked in the factories around here when they first arrived in Southall and some of the factories in Southall are now owned by Punjabi businessmen. When I visited Southall for the first time, it was bustling with people but its atmosphere felt down-at-heel. However, I liked the sign at the train station with the name 'Southall' printed alongside its equivalent in Gurmukhi script.

You could find a lot of things from Punjab in Southall. In fact, the radio station that played Bollywood songs for Punjabi, Gujarati and Bengali audiences in the UK was based in Southall. The Punjabi families who have made it in business in Southall have now moved to other towns, making way for new arrivals. Mosques, Hindu temples and Sikh places of worship, known as *gurdwaras*, are situated not far from each other in Southall.

The word Punjab means a land of five rivers. But the partition of India in 1947 divided the province into two, so there are now two rivers on the Western side and three on the other side of the border in the East. Arif, an acquaintance in London who grew up in a small village near the border in Punjab, told me that sometimes people on the other side of the border would send them packs of *bidis* (small hand-rolled cigarettes wrapped in leaves) tied to the downriver driftwood.

Arif felt at home living in Southall since he could speak Punjabi with many people, from his landlord to the lady who ran a shop below his rented room. His landlord was an elderly Sikh man and Arif got on well with Sikh people because of their common language. His family home was in Lahore but his ancestral home lay in a village outside the city. Arif had come to London for a postgraduate course in Information Technology and worked in a fried chicken shop while studying.

There were a few other tenants living in the building in which he had rented his room in Southall. He was never sure which tenant was next going to receive a knock at the door by officers from the UK Border Force. But no one confided any information about other tenants or their friends living in the building when questioned by the officers. In fact, Arif was one of the few people living in that building who had a valid visa and didn't disappear when these uniformed men and women paid a surprise visit. He worked 72 hours a week to maintain the minimum income requirement for his visa application and paid a big tax bill each year as a self-employed person. He also paid a fee to an accountant for the submission of his tax returns.

Arif was living a frugal existence in a room that he shared with one other person. But he was very generous in lending hard-earned cash to his flatmates and colleagues whenever any of them was in dire straits. For instance, he had become friendly with a Sikh from Canada who was thrown out of his accommodation when he ran out of money. Arif lent him enough to pay his expenses for a couple of weeks until his friend replenished his funds from sources back home. Arif's friends routinely borrowed money from him whenever they needed to pay the large fee required for a visa application.

I wanted to meet Arif's Canadian friend, who was living in a guesthouse in Southall. He had paid five times more for a similar-sized room in a hotel in Central London. Arif respectfully called his friend Shaji, which means 'a King' in Punjabi. He had arranged for me to meet him in a *gurdwara* in Southall. I usually only saw this newly built temple's ribbed gold and white domes from a distance whenever I travelled by cab to Heathrow. It reminded me of a *gurdwara* at the foot of Hari Parbat mountain in Srinagar. I could clearly see its domes whenever I climbed to the top of a mountain in this region. In fact, I always found it very relaxing to listen to Gurbani – the singing of Sikh hymns – in a *gurdwara*.

I met Arif outside the overground train station in Southall and we walked to Havelock Road to meet his friend Shaji in the *gurdwara*. He came to the door to usher us in. Although Shaji didn't wear a turban, he had tied his hair with a black bandana as a mark of respect. We took off our shoes, as is customary when you walk into a *gurdwara* or a mosque. As a child, I had visited the Sikh Golden Temple in Amritsar with my uncle and, at the entrance, handed in my shoes to men with long white beards who looked very respectable. My uncle informed me that some of them were big businessmen who handled shoes as an obligatory mark of humility.

Shaji took us to the main hall of the *gurdwara*, in which a small troupe was singing Gurbani to the accompaniment of a harmonium. There were a few people inside the main hall making their obeisances. Arif and I sat on the floor while Shaji finished praying. He then led us to the *langar* or community kitchen on the lower ground floor of the *gurdwara* and poured tea for us from an urn. The *langars* at *gurdwaras* around the world provide free food for anyone visiting. So *langars* are also frequented by men and women who cannot afford to buy food for themselves. Sikh men and women volunteer to cook food in big cauldrons at a *langar*. When there was a cataclysmic flood in Srinagar in 2014, it was at the *langar* in Amritsar's Golden Temple that thousands of packets of food were prepared and sent to those affected. The word *langar* is used in Kashmiri as a synonym for something that's free of charge. Thus, instead of saying "This isn't a charity shop", an irate businessman might say "This isn't *a langar*". Arif told me that he personally knew two or three people in Southall who were so hard-pressed for money that they went to the *gurdwara* in Havelock Road now and again to have a meal.

The State of Punjab is known as the granary of India

because its land is very fertile and well irrigated. Some Sikh farmers from Punjab have immigrated to America and Canada. However, it was tough for those farmers who couldn't read or write to move to technologically advanced countries in the West. Many of those Sikh men faced discrimination due to their incomprehension of the English language, their uniform headgear and their long beards. However, they bore their hardships with fortitude since Sikh men have always been the butt of jokes in India. I found the Sikh businessmen who came to Srinagar from Ludhiana and Amritsar in Punjab to be lively and good-humoured. But the Sikh men who travelled to the UK and America tended to be less cheerful since they lived solitary lives for many years before they could afford to bring their wives and families over from Punjab.

A few years ago, an elderly Sikh man sat next to me on a flight from London to Delhi. He was travelling from Canada with his wife and had changed planes in London. The couple told me that they lived in a town in Punjab and had travelled to Canada to see their son. He asked me in Urdu if I could ask an airhostess for two small bottles of white wine. After gulping them down, he said that it didn't contain much alcohol and was like drinking vinegar and so he wanted to try a couple of whiskies. But his wife gave him a slap on the wrist, as she didn't want him getting drunk on the plane. Although it is forbidden for Sikhs to drink alcohol they tend to be quite fond of drinking and are more likely to refrain from tobacco.

Shaji had told Arif that he ran an IT company in

Canada. But a few of his projects had fallen through lately and he had run into financial difficulties. He was divorced from his wife and travelled from one country to another in search of new business projects. He had found it beneficial for his spiritual wellbeing to stay near a *gurdwara* in Southall.

Vaisakhi is a celebration of the birth five centuries ago of Khalsa – an order of the Sikh religion – when a group of five men were initiated into Sikhism for the first time. The disciples were forbidden to cut their hair or chew tobacco. They were required to wear a *Kara* (bangle) and carry a sword known as a Kirpan.

I asked Shaji about another *gurdwara* in Southall intriguingly called *Miri-Piri*. He told me that Sikh men carry two Kirpans based on the concept of *Miri-Piri* – a Perso-Arabic word, the first part of which symbolizes temporal and the second part spiritual power. Shaji pointed to an emblem called *Khanda* on a flag outside the *gurdwara* that depicted two Kirpans flanking a double-edged sword. Khalsa was formed as a military brotherhood of Sikhs by Guru Gobind Singh after his father was beheaded by a Mughal Emperor. But the poetry of a Muslim mystic, Baba Farid, is included in the *Guru Granth Sahib* – the Sikh scripture compiled by ten Gurus, the last of whom was himself a poet.

A Sikh man called Gurjet once told VS Naipaul that Amrit, the holy water at Anandpur, which is the birthplace of Khalsa, was stirred by the sword of Ali. Naipaul was bewildered to hear it:

Did he mean the Ali of the Muslim Shias, the cousin and son-in-law of Prophet Mohammed? He did. He said, "The Caliph".

How did the sword survive more than 1000 years? How had it come into the possession of Guru Gobind Singh?

It was presented to him by the Mogul Emperor Bahadur Shah.

I remember a Kashmiri Muslim poet reciting a poem about Amrit on the TV channel, Srinagar Doordarshan, and he received a big round of applause from the Sikhs in the audience.

*

The enterprising spirit of the Sikh community is evident in many towns in India and beyond. I recently met a Sikh businessman in London whose ancestors had travelled overland from Punjab to Siam a century ago and set up a business there. He owned a textile factory in Bangkok and supplied garments to a few big retailers in Europe.

Shaji had heard people in America say that there is no such thing as a free lunch. But it is otherwise, he pointed out, when you enter a *gurdwara*. Of course, I knew he went there to worship rather than to obtain a free meal, but it is customary to eat something at the *langar* when visiting a *gurdwara*. The tall poles with small triangular orange flags known as

Nishan Sahib, on display at Gurdwara Sri Guru Singh Sabha in Havelock Road, reminded me of similar flagpoles that I used to see from far outside the *gurdwara* in Srinagar. The word 'Sahib', by the way, is used respectfully in Punjabi but in Kashmiri it is sometimes used sarcastically, as in 'Lord Sahib', which denotes a bossy person.

The Sikh Empire extended from Mithankot to Kashmir in the 19th Century and when it fell to the British they sold Kashmir to a Maharaja from Jammu for a paltry sum. Perhaps the British believed it would be difficult to rule a remote place like Kashmir where the Kashmiri people were rather too elusive for their Raj. The Sikh Empire of Maharaja Ranjit Singh stretched from Punjab to Khyber. Thousands of Sikhs were living in Afghanistan before Soviet tanks rolled into the country in 1979. Some of the Sikhs from Punjab have travelled as far as Iran and settled in Tehran. In fact, there is a school attached to a *gurdwara* in Tehran where the Punjabi language is taught.

*

And some have ventured as far as Southall. It has become a place of attraction for many people from the Indian subcontinent who visit the UK from other countries in Europe. Its bustle reminds me of Karol Bagh in Delhi where you find shops within shops in the alleyways. You see myriad bolts of colourful cloth behind the shop counters. When I wanted to have a *Shalwar Kurta* garment made a few years ago, the Afghan tailor who alters my trousers in Central London gave me the address of a tailoring workshop in Southall. He told me it was on the upper floor of a certain building. I tried in vain to find the workshop and was obliged to buy a readymade *Shalwar Kurta* at a nearby shop.

Two years ago, a caterer asked me to meet him in his restaurant in Southall for a menu tasting. The restaurant, which was empty during the afternoon, was on the first floor above the shops inside a building on the high street. I sat patiently at a table, expecting a plate of small portions of food to arrive. But in a show of generosity, the caterer had asked his staff to bring a couple of full portions of the dishes on the menu for me. Naturally, the food was prepared on the restaurant's premises. But he also catered for other places and occasions. He used a kitchen in an industrial unit in Wembley to prepare food and then loaded it on a van to take to the venue.

When I went to Wembley for the first time, I found the bases of many of the lampposts in the area had turned a burnt sienna colour. It took me a few more visits there to realise that this was due to the spitting of *Paan* – a mixture of tobacco, nuts and spices wrapped in a leaf. I saw a poster on a wall warning those who spit Paan that they could be fined £80. The Paan chewers in Wembley must have taken a dim view of this poster, however, as they had liberally stained it with their spit.

It is possible to start a business in Southall with a little capital because you need only rent part of a shop rather than the entire premises. My Punjabi landlady usually hired a plumber or an electrician from Southall. The Sikh man who repaired the boiler for her at a reasonable price was born and brought up in Punjab and she was pleased because he had done a very good job.

As a child growing up in Kashmir, I liked to watch the Sikh men from Punjab working skilfully as carpenters. When my uncle wanted a new wardrobe made, he hired two Sikh carpenters from Punjab. I often went over to his home to see how they made the frame for the wardrobe and then covered it with plywood and laminate. I was impressed how well they had made a big wardrobe from scratch. The carpenters and plumbers from Punjab are considered to be better than the local ones in Kashmir. The Sikhs also have good business acumen as small traders. A year ago, I saw some Sikh men on motorbikes, balancing five or six woven-string beds on their bikes, riding from one village to another in the mountainous region of Ladakh. I found it astonishing that they would travel so far to sell their wares in remote Himalayan villages.

I also found a *gurdwara* called Pathar Sahib built on the side of the Leh – Srinagar road. Legend has it that a devil once lived in the mountains there. When the founder of the Sikh religion, Guru Nanak, passed through that place on his way from Tibet to Kashmir, the devil tried to kill him by rolling down a boulder. But the stone had melted and formed a cast of Guru Nanak in a seated pose.

The exterior of the *gurdwara* has been painted in striking orange and blue colours in contrast to the beige landscape. I was surprised to find a Sikh place of worship in the middle of nowhere until a friend accompanying me on the tour told me that even though Guru Nanak had travelled through that place 500 years ago, the shapely stone had only been discovered about 50 years ago. A road was being built and a bulldozer driver realised that he couldn't move a boulder no matter how hard he tried. In the end it snapped the blade of his machine. The driver had a dream that night in which someone told him not to move that stone. I asked my friend if there was a *langar* in Pathar Sahib and he said that there was – in fact a weary traveller could have a cup of tea in this *gurdwara* as well, in Guruji's name.

When I travelled through Punjab as an adolescent, I noticed that the gait of many elderly men and women was lopsided. I assumed that this was due to sitting on a woven-string bed in the open for a long time, rather than other possible factors such as arthritic old age. However, the people in Punjab seemed very industrious to me, since Kashmir is a comparatively laidback place. The State of Punjab has both agriculture and industries and much of what is consumed in Kashmir comes from Punjab. But the people in Kashmir consider their own produce to be organic and hence of special quality, and Punjabi is a generic term for anything imported from outside Kashmir.

I was overwhelmed by the bustle in Amritsar when I visited the city with my uncle. He took me to the home of a factory owner who supplied him with woollen cloth. Our host told us that he used his washing machine for the making of butter. What a *Jugaad*, I thought. People in Kashmir associate the word *Jugaad*, which means ingenuity, with Punjabis who can turn such a thing as a sugarcane juicer running on a diesel engine into a motor vehicle with a sleight of hand. On my way to the school in Srinagar, I liked to watch a Sikh mechanic taking a motorcycle or scooter apart and then paint the body parts anew before assembling them into a motorbike or scooter again. The bodies of buses and trucks in Kashmir were made in workshops in Punjab and decorated according to the wishes of their owners. On a recent visit to Kashmir, I saw a new four-wheel drive vehicle with a pumped up frame. Someone told me it was called Dabwali, after a town of the same name that is located at the border of Punjab and Haryana states. Similarly, people in Kashmir like to call pasteurised milk 'Gurdaspur milk', after a city in Punjab that has a plant for milk processing. And just as every European or American tourist in Kashmir is regarded as English, every domestic tourist, whether from Gujarat or Bengal, is likewise called a Punjabi.

When East Punjab was divided into three states on a linguistic basis two decades after the partition of India, the city of Chandigarh became the joint Capital of Punjab and Haryana. In my student days I heard that Chandigarh was planned by a European architect but didn't realize that the architect was Le Corbusier. Someone who had been to Chandigarh told me it was a well-planned city with parks and gardens. However, I never got a chance to visit Chandigarh since it was an administrative centre rather than an industrial one like Amritsar and Ludhiana. Edwin Lutyens had designed the building in New Delhi in the neo-classical style whereas Le Corbusier designed the building in Chandigarh in the raw concrete style of modern architecture.

Whenever I travelled by road from Srinagar to Delhi I was apprehensive about passing through Pathankot, which lies at the border where Punjab meets Jammu and Kashmir. Coaches would leave Srinagar in the morning and drive along a mountainous terrain until they reached Jammu in the evening, eventually arriving at Pathankot late at night. The traffic would come to a halt at Pathankot as all the vehicles were checked for taxable goods passing from one state into another. There was usually a long line of trucks waiting to clear the checkpoint. Although the distance between Srinagar and Delhi is only 500 miles, in those days it took 24 hours – without replacement drivers – to cover that distance by coach or car. Because the coaches drove through Punjab during the night and reached Delhi in the morning, both passengers and drivers were utterly exhausted and somewhat the worse for wear.

It was in the early 1980s that video-equipped coaches were introduced on this route. These coaches seemed very luxurious as their windows had curtains to keep the light out during the day while passengers watched Bollywood films. I was keen to experience one of those coaches and one day got a chance to travel in one from Srinagar to Delhi. However, the coach's engine constantly interfered with the playing of the tape in the VCR, resulting in a heavily scrambled screen image and a crackling sound. I wished the film would stop so I didn't have to listen to the awful noise but other passengers were engrossed in it and seemed oblivious to the disturbance. I marvelled how these people could escape into the fantasy world of a Bollywood film amid such noise. It was bad enough to see half of the small television screen covered by a running banner of adverts. It didn't bother my fellow passengers, though, who were enthralled to see the matinee idol, Dilip Kumar, playing the role of a law-abiding citizen who turns to crime. The drivers of these 'luxury' coaches pulled up outside their favourite Dhaba (a roadside food stall) for a meal or a snack during the 24-hour ride. I tried to go to the Dhaba on the opposite side of the road but was stopped by a waiter who told me that as I had used their washroom I must dine with them.

*

I haven't been to Southall again to see a Vaisakhi Mela in mid-April. This festival is now celebrated in other towns of the UK, from Trafalgar Square in London to Old Market Square in Nottingham. I recently went to Nottingham to see a friend and found a big marquee pitched in the town square for the celebration of Vaisakhi. It was closing time but there were still a few people sitting inside the marquee in front of the *Guru Granth Sahib Ji* – the holy book of Sikhs. A group of Sikh men were practising *Gatka*, a form of sword-fighting martial art.

In a smaller marquee a Sikh man was showing an Englishman how to tie a turban. It is really an art to tie six yards of cloth into a turban. Many people find it complicated to knot a tie, let alone tie a turban stylishly around their head. My (non-Sikh) grandfather would neatly fold a long muslin cloth before tying it around a brimless hat on his head. He took off his turban when he sat in his shop and when he came home in the evening. In Kashmir, a bridegroom usually wore a green turban on his wedding day as part of his attire. You could rent the headgear for a wedding from a barber in Srinagar who always kept a crisp turban ready in a glass cabinet.

Sikhs are considered to be more martial than other people in Northern India. The East India Company had formed a Sikh regiment even before the fall of the Sikh Empire. It was the Sikh General, Zorawar Singh, who made Ladakh part of the Sikh Empire and perhaps that is why he is also known as Bonaparte.

The Sikh Regiment was co-opted as an infantry regiment of the Indian Army after independence was achieved in 1947. Those Sikhs who had collaborated with the British in crushing the 1857 Mutiny were seen as traitors, and ill will towards Sikhs became palpable after the partition of India, which in turn gave rise to their demand for a separate homeland.

In the early 1980s this demand heightened and became headline news. The militants operated from the sanctum of the Golden Temple in Amritsar. In the evening I would tune my small portable radio to the BBC World Service to find out what was going on since All India Radio didn't give much away by way of news. It was during this period that I missed an interview for attending a winter sports course at the Gulmarg resort. When I went to the office of the organisers to enquire about it, a crusty official informed me that the date had been announced on a local TV Channel, adding sarcastically that perhaps I listened to the BBC instead. As a matter of fact, I did and could therefore only lower my head.

The militants who called the shots from the inside of the Golden Temple were killed in a massive army operation. It came to light many years later that a British SAS officer was drafted in to advise the Indian authorities how to conduct this assault. It was Prime Minister Indira Gandhi who had ordered the army to storm the temple. Since I had visited the temple a few years earlier with my uncle, I felt bereft when I heard the news about the building: Its interior was utterly destroyed. Operation Blue Star, as it was named, caused resentment among Sikhs serving in the Indian Army, some of whom returned medals awarded for their gallantry. A few months after the army operation, when I switched on my portable radio around noon, I heard that Indira Gandhi had been shot dead by her Sikh bodyguards. There was rioting in Delhi and other cities and thousands of Sikh men and women were killed. A lot of property looted from Sikh homes, such as TVs and VCRs, was sold openly after the riots.

Arif wanted me to try some food at a restaurant in Southall that bore the name of his hometown, Lahore. He insisted that I should have something to eat there. I was familiar with the name of the restaurant since there was a branch not far from my place of work in London. Although I wasn't hungry I couldn't bring myself to say no to Arif since he is a very hospitable person. He told me the restaurant had a big turnover of customers throughout the day. He ordered some food that arrived in no time.

While we ate, I asked Arif about his plans for the future and he said that he wanted to go back to live in Lahore. He had got married a couple of years before. His wife had lived in Southall with him for a year and then returned to their family home where she had given birth to a baby girl. Arif told me that his mother wasn't well and needed their support. Besides, he had had enough of his home-to-work and work-to-home routine while living in the UK. He had recently obtained his British passport but the will to live in the UK indefinitely was gone. He said it was beyond his means to buy a small place in Middlesex. And besides, he didn't want to raise a family in a small room. His father, who had passed away 20 years ago, had left a big house for his family in Lahore.

I asked Arif what it was like to live in Southall and commute to work in Central London. He said that he could find everything from Punjab in Southall, especially his favourite fruit, mangoes. They had many mango trees on their ancestral land in a village outside Lahore. But he found more varieties of mangoes, from Alphonso to Kesar, on sale in Southall than in his hometown. Most of the restaurants in Southall were inexpensive and it was easy to take a bus from there to Heathrow whenever he travelled to Lahore.

Although I had seen aircraft flying very low, one after another, over West Hounslow station and had often wondered how people living in the area coped with the constant noise in the skies above them, it hadn't actually occurred to me that there could be some advantage in living near an airport.

This close proximity must similarly have given a sanguine hope to the Sikh men who settled here 60 years ago that if the worst came to the worst they could always jump on a nearby plane and go home.

The Art of Seeing

A few weeks after my arrival in London I drifted into the National Gallery in Trafalgar Square. As it was, and still is, free to visit, I was to look around it whenever I roamed the streets in the City of Westminster. But that initial occasion was actually the first time that I had been inside any art gallery and therefore couldn't distinguish the works of one painter from another. However, it was truly a feast for my eyes to look at the pictures on the gallery walls. A few months later a friend of my father visited me in London and I took him for an impromptu walk around the National Gallery. He was overawed by the paintings and the gallery and wondered what my father would make of it when he told him about our detour.

After becoming acquainted with the National Gallery I began to discover other galleries in London. A few of the Londoners I'd got to know were surprised that I could happily hop from one gallery to another as they found it tedious to visit even one of them in their home town. I thought it strange that someone would miss a great art exhibition on their own doorstep when others travel from distant places to see it. However, I have since fallen into the habit of other Londoners and tend to take all art exhibitions in the town for granted, usually deciding to go and see one when it is already over. However, I am inclined to see an art exhibition if I happen to visit another European city like Berlin or Barcelona because I am often inspired by people I meet at our hotel who have travelled from other countries expressly to see an exhibition.

During my first few months in London, I would hear people describing this painting or that as 'Impressionist' or 'expressionist', and one day I asked a young woman customer whom I had met in the Hampstead corner shop where I worked, and whose mother taught at a college of art, to explain the difference between these two movements. In truth, I was attracted to this customer.

A few years later when Tate Modern hosted an exhibition of Turner's paintings, I mentioned to this woman, who had since married, that I planned to see it and she said she'd like to join me. How I'd longed for her to accompany me to see an exhibition or a film during the time before she married. She lived in a neighbouring street called Courthope Road, a nice irony given that my flatmate had bluntly expressed his opinion that I didn't have the slightest hope of courting her. But now that she was married and assumed that I must have finally got over my crush, she was willing to see an exhibition with me.

I had been fascinated to see a poster of *The Fighting Temeraire* by JMW Turner in the National Gallery shop. I wasn't familiar with the historical event that Turner's painting depicted but I was captivated by the warm orange of his setting sun. Derek Walcott's father, Warwick, had left a copy of Turner's painting for his son before his death. Writing about his father's apprenticeship as an amateur painter, Walcott comments, 'Learning didn't betray his race if he copied a warship's final berth, a cinder in a Turner sunset burning.'

Turner is said to have anticipated Impressionism by dissolving form in the colour in his paintings. But I felt so wretched on seeing Turner's watercolours and drawings in the company of my former customer that I regretted not going to the Tate on my own. In my room in Hampstead I had pinned up a poster of a painting by Manet in which a waitress serves drinks in The Brasserie de Reichshoffen in Paris, a young woman whom I thought resembled the one who accompanied me to the Tate. Why on earth had I agreed to go to see an exhibition with someone who had rejected me?

During my first few years in London I usually filled my weekends by going to a museum or art gallery and I used to frequent the Southbank Centre on Sundays to sit in a coffee shop in its foyer. I was surprised to discover a poetry library on the 5th floor of the Festival Hall. Bookshops in London usually have only a small section allocated to poetry books. The Southbank Centre, at least, has dedicated an entire library to works of poetry. And commendably they try to acquire three copies of every book: one shelf copy for visitors to read in the library, one to go out on loan, and one spare.

There was a dearth of libraries in Srinagar when I was a student. I had found only three or four in our town of more than half a million people. Luckily, one of them was part of a museum and had a quiet reading room but no one ever set foot in it. The other one was in my own neighbourhood, located above the shops in a busy street.

On one occasion I was sitting in the foyer of the Southbank Centre with my nose in a book when a woman suddenly stood before me, asked me if she could sit on an adjoining chair and then proceeded to tell me with a straight face how much she detested the author whose book I was reading. A few seconds later she whispered that her son was having an incestuous relationship. She seemed to be very frank about it but I wasn't sure if she was crazy or telling me the truth. She bumped into me again a few weeks later near Hampstead Heath but I didn't allow myself to be drawn into conversation with her in case she confided something even more disturbing.

Sometimes I would walk from the Southbank Centre to the Hayward Gallery and browse the rows of second-hand bookstalls on the way. It was before a giant Ferris wheel was erected and thousands of tourists would descend on the South Bank every day to take a ride on what was perhaps named by a marketing man as the London Eye. It took me a decade and a half after it was built to persuade myself to take a ride on it.

The new millennium saw a landmark building that loomed large over the Thames turned into an art gallery.

I had seen the big brick building on Bankside many times and was glad that an old power station was going to be used as a modern art gallery. In fact, I hadn't entered a gallery that exhibited modern art until I visited the Tate Modern. On my first visit to the Tate, I was more impressed by Giles Gilbert Scott's architectural brickwork than the works of modern art hanging on the walls. The Turbine Hall was devoid of big generators, but a giant spider made of steel crawled along the floor. As a child, I was curious how electricity was produced in a power plant and one day walked into a hydroelectric station outside Srinagar. I had seen the lengthy pipes attached at a steep angle to an adjoining mountainside but didn't realise how fast the water moved the turbines inside the hall, so much so that the wheels had to be constantly oiled.

By the time I visited Tate Modern again, after a gap of nearly two decades, it had become one of the most visited modern art galleries in the world. I found that another building in latticed brickwork had arisen next to it by way of an extension. Many of the gallery's visitors are now heading straight to the 10th floor to gaze not on paintings and sculptures but on panoramic views of London. The cityscape has altered since the Tate Modern first opened its doors to the public and there are now skyscrapers of all shapes and sizes surrounding the building.

A sign on the viewing gallery requests visitors to respect the privacy of the neighbours who work or live in the high-rise buildings around the Tate and choose not to curtain the glass walls of their homes and offices. When I visited, security guards were keeping a watchful eye on the viewing gallery where, I was shocked to learn, a little boy had been thrown off the building by a disturbed teenager a couple of weeks before.

I descended the stairs to see the artworks displayed on each floor and discovered Matisse's vivid cut-outs on one of the floors. I liked his vibrant artworks very much. I had cut a postcard of one of his paintings into two and used the two halves as bookmarks for many years. I had also bought a black and white picture postcard of Henri Matisse, photographed at his home by Henri Cartier-Bresson. He is wearing a white turban and a matching beard, and drawing a pigeon held gently in his left hand. When a friend saw that photograph on a wall in my home in Kashmir, he mistook Matisse for my grandfather, who also sported a white turban and a white beard. On another occasion, while visiting the National Portrait Gallery, I stumbled upon Henri Cartier-Bresson's photos taken in Kashmir.

While working in the West End of London, I sometimes walked into the Photographer's Gallery during my lunch-break to see the photos on display or browse in its bookshop. This offered me a kind of escape from my humdrum daily working life. And my stroll along Charing Cross Road would usually come to a halt outside a shop selling books on art. The big hardbacks on display in their dust jackets looked more like posters.

In March 2001, when I began working in a London

hotel, I met a guest who had come to London particularly to see an exhibition, *Vermeer and the Delft School*, at the National Gallery. He told me that it was quite hard to obtain a ticket for this exhibition. I felt inspired by Proust, who describes Vermeer's work in his epic novel, *In Search of Lost Time*, and determined to see his paintings. Luckily it wasn't too busy when I walked into the National Gallery in the afternoon and was offered a ticket to view in an hour's time.

In a letter to a friend, Proust declares:

> The original painter proceeds on the lines of the oculist to create the visual world afresh for us and the artist of genius could be inspired by commonplace models. As soon as I first set eyes on the *View of Delft* in the Hague Museum, I knew that I had seen the most beautiful picture in the world. In *Swann's Way* I could not resist the temptation to make Swann plan a study of Vermeer ... though at that time I knew very little about Vermeer ... this artist who keeps his back to us, who set no store upon being seen by posterity, and who will never know what posterity thinks of him, moves me profoundly.

Proust and Vermeer seem to have a lot in common as artists. Vermeer's masterpieces depict paintings within paintings just as Proust's masterwork consists of six related volumes. Proust rendered his use of language precious through endless refinements just as Vermeer made subtle use of the celestial blue element of ultramarine. If Vermeer is a painter of the female universe then Proust is its poet. Proust immortalised Francoise, Aunt Leonie's cook, in his work just as Vermeer made a milkmaid into an allegorical figure. Vermeer made use of a camera obscura because it shows reality undistorted, just as Proust found memory to be the only valid source for his narrative. And the narrator in Proust's work remains hidden, like the artist in Vermeer's studio whose back is turned to the viewer.

Proust had seen the *View of Delft* for the first time in 1902 at Mauritshuis and knew this painting by heart. It was given on loan to the exhibition of Dutch paintings held in Paris in 1921 when the whole town flocked to see it. Proust decided to leave his cork-lined room, well-groomed as usual, to see the exhibition, and it was there that Proust had a presentiment of his own death. From the events of that day Proust truthfully draws in his novel the scene of the death of a writer while contemplating a Vermeer painting:

> His dizziness increased; he fixed his gaze, like a child upon a yellow butterfly that it wants to catch, on the precious little patch of wall . . . In a celestial pair of scales there appeared to him, weighing down one of his pans, his own

life, while the other contained the little patch of wall so beautifully painted in yellow. He felt that he had rashly sacrificed the former for the latter.

The novelist, Bergotte, tries to redeem his soul in Proust's novel while the author imagines regaining his lost time.

Proust imagines meeting John Ruskin as an elderly man at a Rembrandt exhibition in Amsterdam. He was nearing the end of his life and yet he had travelled a long distance to see Rembrandt's paintings.

Blackened like Rembrandt by the shadow of nightfall, by the patina of time, by the obliterating years, he was still led on by the same endeavour to understand beauty. It certainly seemed that the Rembrandt canvases had grown worthier to be visited since Ruskin, from so far away, had come into the room; it seemed too that for Rembrandt this was like a reward which he might have found sweet, and that if his gaze which seemed to be studying us out of the depth of his consummated pictures had been able to see Ruskin, the master would have been at his service, like a king who recognises a king among the crowd.

Vermeer remained obscure for hundreds of years but then at the beginning of the 20th century received recognition when one of the greatest writers of the age became his fervent admirer.

It was two decades ago that someone I knew in Hampstead visited Holland and brought me back a captivating postcard of a *lacemaker* completely absorbed in her work – a feminine occupation that goes back to biblical times. It was Vermeer's Lacemaker that Renoir considered to be one of the two finest paintings in the Louvre. However, it wasn't on display at the exhibition in the National Gallery.

I saw *Vermeer and the Delft School* exhibition at the National Gallery in its third week when the initial rush had subsided and there were no queues at the ticket counters. I found myself mainly among elderly people who, compared with younger visitors, moved from picture to picture and room to room at a pleasingly unhurried pace.

When I entered the first room, the masters of the Delft School carried me to an earlier era in their scenes of everyday life. The summer heat felt cooled by the aspen green walls of the exhibition rooms and the pictures on the walls came to life, casting a spell on me.

I walked into another room and was startled to see a large painting of a courtesan and a procuress. It brought to my mind a poem by Baudelaire in *Flowers of Evil*. The innocent expression of the courtesan contrasts with the sinister grin of the procuress. One of the two men in the painting has a hand on the courtesan's breast and he is holding a coin in his other hand. The other man in the painting – thought by some to be

Vermeer himself – seems to be a musician. Renoir travelled from Bayreuth to Dresden especially to see this painting.

The next two rooms displayed the works of Pieter de Hooch and Carel Fabritius, including *The Courtyard of a House in Delft*. The neatness of the courtyard is suggested in the painting by a pail and a broom.

The last room displayed only the paintings of Vermeer, to honour Delft's greatest painter. Proust writes:

> Vermeer's paintings were fragments of an identical world, that is always, however great the genius with which they have been recreated, the same table, the same carpet, the same woman, the same novel and unique beauty, an enigma, at that epoch in which nothing resembles or explains it, if one doesn't try to relate it all through subject matter but to isolate the distinctive impression produced by the colour.

It was difficult to leave that room. I could do so only by telling myself that I would return to see it again.

One of Vermeer's paintings, *The Guitar Player*, hangs on a wall in Kenwood House, the usual destination of my walks through Hampstead Heath. Although I sometimes strolled into Kenwood House I couldn't remember seeing it there. However, I read in the newspapers about its theft a long time ago and how it was eventually found abandoned in a cemetery.

The Hampstead corner shop that I worked in sold postcards by The Medici Society and it was these very colourful cards that familiarized me with the works of various painters. I was surprised to read the following description on one of these cards when I turned it over: 'He painted like an apprentice who was going to be sacked: name of the artist – Picasso.' I became fond of Picasso's drawings and even copied his *War and Peace* using tracing paper. A decade and a half later, while roaming the streets around Las Ramblas in Barcelona with a friend, I sneaked into the Picasso Museum to see paintings produced during various periods in his life, while my friend waited for me in a nearby Tapas bar. However, when I travelled to Malaga with some friends, I didn't get to see the Picasso Museum in the town of his birth.

I once chose a poster of a Picasso painting in a shop near the Louvre in Paris and when I went to the counter to pay for it, the shopkeeper asked me for 10 euros, whereas the price displayed was 20 euros. When I mentioned it to the shopkeeper he looked at me in disbelief, handed me a key-ring with a miniature Eiffel Tower attached to it and said, "This is for your honesty." I liked his pronunciation of the word 'honesty,' which included the letter 'h'.

I carried the poster in a tube to Kashmir with a view to having it framed for display in a room in my parents' home. My nephew drove me to a framing shop in Srinagar. A few days later when I went to collect my poster from the framer, I was dismayed to see that he had done a bad job. I asked him politely to charge me for his work but make a new frame for me. He was infuriated, extracted the poster brusquely from the frame, thrust it into my hand and challenged me to find a better framer than him in the town. When I failed to find another framer I rolled up the poster and put it in a tube to carry back to London with me.

*

Tate Modern has stolen the limelight from Tate Britain in the last two decades. So it was welcome news for me to hear that Tate Britain was hosting an exhibition on Van Gogh. I had even forgotten how to get there from the Tube station.

Van Gogh's paintings are considered to be post-impressionist, and, according to Derek Walcott, the artists who started Impressionism – Monet, Pissarro et al – had a horror of the beautiful. Their works were at first rejected by the established salons and galleries but later constituted a school of art in themselves. Van Gogh was influenced by English literature when he lived in London and wrote to his brother: 'Reading books is like looking at paintings . . . one must find beautiful that which is beautiful.' Among the selection of books on display at the Van Gogh exhibition at the Tate was a copy of *Keats' Poetical Works.* He also liked reading Dickens and says, 'My whole life is aimed at making the things from everyday life that Dickens describes.'

Van Gogh spent three years in England and worked for an art dealer. Influenced by a handful of British artists, he himself inspired generations of artists in Britain and elsewhere. I was surprised to learn at the exhibition that Van Gogh was influenced by the English painter, John Constable. I had found Constable's painting of Hampstead Heath dull compared to *Wheat Fields* by Van Gogh. Van Gogh had also influenced The Camden Group of post-impressionist painters. Camille Pissarro's son, Lucien, was a member of this group for some time. I saw his *La Maison de la Sourde, Éragny* at the exhibition and realised that the younger Pissarro, though his grey rabbinical beard made him resemble his father, was an accomplished painter in his own right.

A display of black and white pictures at the Tate entitled *How I love London* made me aware of my own love affair with the city. Van Gogh had worked for an art dealer in Covent Garden. When I first arrived in London I spent much of my time in Covent Garden before starting to work on my first book while sitting in a coffee shop in Camden Town. Van Gogh was dismissed from his job after two years and tried to pursue a life of religious service, his brother, Theo, suggesting that he take up art when he failed as a pastor. I lost my job in a corner shop near Keats House in London after two years.

Van Gogh was an admirer of John Keats and considered him to be a fine painter with words. He copied out Keats's poem, *To Autumn*, and like the poet himself, autumn became his favourite season in the landscapes he painted. He thought nature was 'more serious and intimate' in autumn just as Keats found it to be a 'season of mists and mellow fruitfulness'. Van Gogh had seen Constable's *The Valley Farm* in South

Kensington Museum and wrote to his brother that he kept thinking about a couple of very fine Constables, referring to *The Cornfield* and *The Valley Farm*.

The room at Tate Britain that displayed Van Gogh's *Starry Night Over the Rhône* was crowded and many visitors were taking selfies in front of it. The painting was borrowed from the Musée d'Orsay. I have passed that museum in Paris many times but never got a chance to look around inside. I did spend an afternoon in the nearby Louvre on my second visit to Paris only to find *Mona Lisa* luring everyone towards her wing of the museum. I was glad to see the *Starry Night* at last, conveniently on display at a gallery in my own town.

The variety of paintings on display was exhilarating. Van Gogh's oil paintings burst with colour. However, *Carpenters Yard and Laundry* is like an engraving. The swirls of colour in *Starry Night* are these days seen by students of science as an illustration of fluid dynamics. And of all the pictures, I found Van Gogh's sketch of *Sorrowing Old Man* with his head in his hands to be the most haunting.

There was a painting of Victoria Embankment by De Nittis on display at the exhibition. When Van Gogh saw that painting in Paris, he realised how much he loved London. He crossed Westminster Bridge often and liked to see the sun setting behind the Houses of Parliament. Monet has painted a series of pictures of Westminster and I particularly like his *Thames Below Westminster*. He obscured the Houses of Parliament in his paintings. I bought a poster of Monet's painting to take with me to Kashmir. But, not daring to take it to the crusty framer in Srinagar, I simply pinned it to the door of a room in my parents' home. I took it down myself a year ago because my father was about to move home and I didn't want him to tear it.

It was a portrait of an unclothed seamstress hiding her head in her arms that I found most affecting at the Tate exhibition. The portrait depicts Sien Hoornick, who, when he met her, had 'one foot in the grave' according to Van Gogh. He took her in, along with her daughter, despite the disapproval of his relatives. It is a tender portrait of a woman in desperate circumstances. I mistook the subject's baby bump for flab when I first saw the portrait but learnt later that she was pregnant when she modelled for Van Gogh. He told his brother in a letter that she has been abandoned by the man whose child she was carrying. He felt moved by the poor conditions of seamstresses in general, depicting another of them in his watercolour, *Woman Sewing and Cat.*

The men moving in a circle in Van Gogh's *The Prison Courtyard*, also on display in the Tate Britain's exhibition, brought Dante's *Inferno* to mind. The painter believed it was the prison of poverty and social prejudice that prevented him from becoming the artist he wanted to be. He had found the prices of pictures by dead painters dizzying. But it is difficult for young unknown artists to recoup the expenses of their craft.

An elegant portrait of Van Gogh's friend, Marie Ginoux, who ran a coffee shop at a train station in Arles, hung at the entrance of the exhibition like a maître d'hôtel welcoming you in; and the artist's self-portrait with paintbrushes in hand bade you farewell at the end of the exhibition. However, it was *The Sunflowers*, which had travelled a few miles down the road from the National Gallery, that awaited visitors before they departed from the Tate. I had seen it many years ago and felt it had increased in beauty since then. A vintage poster in the shop informed me that Tate Britain had hosted an exhibition of Van Gogh's paintings before, in 1947, a resonant date for me as this was the very year in which the jewel in the crown, India, had gained independence from Britain.

I left the Tate and walked along Millbank to reach the bus stop. It was evening and I saw a jumble of commuters on their bikes heading home. The bus took a detour but my mind was still wandering through Van Gogh's vivid landscapes and the town of Arles.

*

There are so many museums and galleries in London that visiting all of them can keep you occupied for many months. I haven't yet visited Dulwich Picture Gallery, which established even before Van Gogh came to live in London. You can find his name in an early volume of its visitors' books. I hope one day to venture as far afield as Dulwich to see this historic gallery.

I had bought a poster of *The Stonemason's Yard* by Canaletto at the National Gallery shop and hung it above the fireplace to liven up my solitary room in Hampstead.

I had much admired a panoramic view of Venice painted by Canaletto, with boats being rowed up and down. So I was somewhat underwhelmed when I visited the so-called 'Little Venice' in London, having expected something much grander. But on the other hand, when I visited Greenwich, I found that a splendid view of the Royal Naval Hospital from the river thoroughly merited Canaletto's painting of the scene.

It was astonishing to learn how many European artists, from Monet to Pissarro, had made London their home for a time and who painted houses and gardens in the town on their canvasses. They made use of light to create their masterpieces of this pearl-grey city. In fact, I found their paintings more evocative of London than Turner's sunsets.

London has offered refuge to writers and painters alike. Voltaire and Zola lived in exile in London. Monet and Pissarro toured the museums together. The light in London may not be the same as in Giverny and Arles but Monet was very productive when he lived in London and Van Gogh spent three formative years in the town.

It was only after touring museums and galleries in London that I realised how all the great masters have suffered for their art. But sadly, in our brashly commercial age, some of our celebrated artists behave more like the businessmen who give lectures to students in the London School of Business on how to re-invent themselves. Art and advertising seem to have converged into one form. Looking at the great works of Vermeer and Van Gogh gave me courage to press on with my writing and set no store by any returns for my endeavours in pursuit of a vocation. I also realised the truth in Derek Walcott's poetry when he states that the ancient war between obsession and responsibility will never finish. In my view, it was Walcott's failure as a painter that enabled him to become a great poet.

Proust knew well that second-rate writers earned more than him from their writing and yet he spent his last *sou* on sustaining his obsession of writing in a cork-lined room and buying flowers for society women. I feel grateful to Proust for introducing me to the works of Vermeer and Baudelaire and I would go as far as saying that the most memorable year for me in London was the one in which I read Proust's *In Search of Lost Time*. It helped to make London a liveable town for me.

❧

Travelling to Kashmir

I was planning to travel to Kashmir from London in February 2019 to visit my parents when news broke that the airspace above it was closed after a dogfight between Indian and Pakistani warplanes. In fact, 'planning' is the wrong verb to use when it comes to travelling to a restive place like Srinagar. So my sanguine hope was that travelling to Kashmir in August to celebrate the Islamic Festival of Eid with my parents would have a better chance of peaceful conditions. I booked my tickets to Srinagar two months earlier in London to fly there from New Delhi on the 5th of August.

Some of my friends and relatives warned me a few days before I was due to land in Srinagar that I should put my visit to Kashmir on hold because, when thousands of troops were sent to the Valley, they foresaw that a calamity was going to befall the region. However, a couple of other friends suggested it might be nothing and I should board my flight, as scheduled.

I had decided to stop over in Gurgaon near Delhi for a few days, en route to Kashmir. A friend who lives near Lake Dal rang me on the 4th of August to say that foreign tourists staying in the hotels and houseboats in his neighbourhood had been visited by security forces who ordered them to leave Srinagar. I rang the airline and to my surprise they cancelled my ticket without asking me the reason for it. In 2016, in contrast, I'd had endless trouble with British Airways in trying to cancel my ticket from London to Delhi, and in the end I flew into Srinagar when there was a continuous 72-hour curfew in the town. It took me exactly that long to reach my parents' home which was hardly 10 miles away from the airport. They have since moved much closer to the airport; but when I spoke to my mother on the phone from Gurgaon prior to 5th August, she wasn't keen that I visit her this time when the situation in Kashmir was so dire.

I met a Kashmiri friend for dinner in Gurgaon on the eve of the 5th August. He feared there was going to be a massive army operation in Kashmir, causing such panic among the population that they were stocking up with food and medicine in their homes.

I had arranged with friends in Srinagar to make a trip to the distant Himalayan valley of Gurez. I have always found its remoteness very alluring. It remains cut off for several months of the year due to heavy snowfall and it had snowed there as late as June this year. A friend in Montreal had sent me a newspaper feature on Gurez a year earlier and I was determined to go there on my next visit to Kashmir.

Unfortunately, my last two trips to Kashmir were due to bereavements in the family. I hinted to a relative that peace was elusive in Kashmir and he retorted that it was rather insensitive of me to think of travelling to the paradise that is Gurez through Kashmir where all hell was going to break loose. For many months, I had dreamed of pitching a tent on the banks of the River Kishanganga and breathing some pure mountain air, which – according to the Swiss – can make you slim.

I heard the news about skirmishes at the so-called Line of Control in Gurez, which had been relatively peaceful in the few days before I flew from London to Delhi. This was not a good omen. But I had cycled more than 10 miles from my home to Central London on the hottest day ever recorded in the UK to buy camping gear at Mountain Warehouse, so I was reluctant to give up my plan. A trip to Zanskar in Ladakh had given me a fair idea about the essentials for camping on the banks of a mountain stream, but I still sought the help of a shop assistant to buy the right equipment. He told me that an ordinary backpack would do if I was just going away for a weekend, but if I needed it for trekking in the Himalayas it had to be both more robust and more lightweight.

When I awoke on the morning of 5th of August, I discovered that the phone lines in Kashmir had been cut during the night. This preceded the official announcement of the bifurcation of Jammu and Kashmir and the downgrading of the state into two Union Territories, thereby revoking Article 370 of the Indian constitution, which had granted Kashmir a special status. The communication blockade in Kashmir seems to have come full circle in the last 30 years.

In 1990 I had to travel 500 miles from Srinagar to Delhi to make an overseas phone call.

It became clear by midmorning on the 5th of August that the stories about insurgents trying to cross the de facto border in Kashmir were a pretext for sending thousands of troops to Kashmir to suppress any uprising after the revoking of Article 370.

I chose to stay in Gurgaon without a TV set, in order to take a break from the 24-hour news bulletins. However, I informed my friends in London and elsewhere that I hadn't travelled to Srinagar and was staying in Gurgaon for longer than I had intended, so they shouldn't worry about me when watching the news about the clampdown in Kashmir. A friend emailed me to inform me that, according to Wikipedia, Gurgaon has earned the dubious accolade of being the most polluted city in the world (though other sources accord this status to New Delhi). However, the bright city lights and a luminescent crescent in the dark sky over New Gurgaon evoked the scene of *A Starry Night over the Rhone* in my mind. Van Gogh was inspired to paint his *Starry Night* picture by a scenic view of the Thames. Perhaps the air in Victorian London was more polluted than the Millennium-created city of Gurgaon.

Driving through Gurgaon in a cab at night, you find big shops selling 'English Beer and Wine'. In fact, the wines sold there might be from anywhere in the world, but 'English' is a generic term used for imported drinks that were known as

'Vilayati' during the Raj. And the corruption of this word is 'Blighty' – a nostalgic term used by Englishmen and women during the British Empire era to denote their mother country. These liquor shops in Gurgaon can be spotted from afar by bright lights hung like bunting in their forecourts.

During the afternoon of the 5th of August I visited a hardware shop in Gurgaon, feeling very downhearted. The owner of the shop, having recognised me as someone from Kashmir, asked me my opinion of the revocation of Article 370. I went to another shop and a few people sitting around there expressed their pleasure at the news of the day. I took a cab to the nearest Metro station, which was miles away. The cabdriver jumped a red light in haste but was immediately pulled over by a cop. There were two more cops standing on the side of the road behind a few rags hanging from a clothesline. The driver took a wallet from his back pocket and approached the cops, who were screened from my view by the clothesline.

When the driver returned, I asked him if they wanted to see his driving licence. He replied that they just wanted a bribe of 200 rupees. So much for corruption in Kashmir, cited as one of the reasons for the revocation of Article 370 by politicians in New Delhi. My cab fare was 250 rupees, out of which the driver had also paid a toll of 60 rupees. I estimated that, having paid off the cops, the poor driver would end up with precious little for driving me such a long distance, so I decided to reimburse him.

The Metro station was brimming with people and I joined a long queue to be frisked at its entrance. A man from Rajasthan standing behind me struck up a conversation about the goings-on in Kashmir. He wanted to know if I was related to any politician there. I usually find the London Underground gloomy because commuters keep their heads down and generally don't talk to strangers. But I would have preferred to be travelling in a London Tube train on this occasion. The next day I saw a newspaper advert for a company that makes dairy products, gleefully celebrating the revocation of Article 370.

It rained frequently in Gurgaon during my stay in the town, bringing the level of air pollution down, and the newspapers reported for two consecutive days that the air quality was good, which is a rarity in Delhi and Gurgaon. I found more butterflies fluttering in Gurgaon than I have seen in any other town, and I even heard birdsong in the morning. Yet I still yearned for the cool mountain air of Kashmir.

In the meantime, businesses in Gurgaon were going into overdrive in preparation for Independence Day, celebrating the historic handover by the British Raj. Some of them were offering a discount of 47% to celebrate freedom from colonial rule in 1947 and others were offering as much as 72% to match the number of years since India has become a sovereign country. These celebrations have now turned into one big commercial enterprise. However, the celebration of Eid in Kashmir was this year a relatively muted affair. It is customary in Kashmir for Eid to be a sombre occasion if there is bereavement in the family, and the demise of Article 370 a few days before the Eid gave people a reason for not celebrating the festival at all. In the words of an Urdu poet, 'How could I celebrate Eid, when I am bereaved?'

Kashmir has everything to lure the intrepid traveller, and all it requires as a destination is a climate of peace. But the revocation of Article 370 has diminished the chances of that. The Governor of Jammu and Kashmir tried to assure people in Srinagar at the beginning of August that it was only a rumour that Article 370 was going to be revoked, with a caveat that he didn't know what was going to happen tomorrow. It was an unsurprising statement, though, from New Delhi's own man in Kashmir. It was always Jammu and Kashmir that was in the news, with Ladakh as its backwater. But now the state has been sliced into two and Ladakh seems as big as Jammu and Kashmir. I was thrilled when a white colleague in London revealed to me that his last name was Ladakh. And an Englishman once told me that he only learned that Kashmir was officially called Jammu and Kashmir in the singular when he became acquainted with the political map of the region. Some English people actually confuse Kashmir with Nepal, which is also a mountainous territory. But confusion abounds in this geopolitical region – a legacy of the British Raj.

*

I always feel enticed by the mountains. It is an old urge. Perhaps it has to do with my growing up in Kashmir where the Himalayas, Karakoram and Hindukush meet. I had visited Ladakh for the first time three decades ago with some friends. We flew to Leh from Srinagar and travelled by road on our way back, stopping halfway at Kargil for a night.

Kargil has become synonymous with war since the breaking out of hostilities between India and Pakistan in 1999. I was horrified when I read newspaper reports in London that the two countries were capable of using thermonuclear weapons in that war. One of the reports highlighted how many millions would be killed in the event of such a conflict in the subcontinent. I rang my mother but she seemed oblivious of the impending danger and told me it was business as usual in Srinagar.

It didn't take long after the war, though, for Kargil to be on the tourist map again. In fact, some people travelled to Kargil to see the mountains where the recent battles were fought. In the meantime, some of the guidebooks on India omitted chapters on Kashmir in their updated editions. Some years later a new road opened connecting Leh with Manali, making it possible to travel to Ladakh from Delhi and other cities in India without passing through Srinagar. Someone I met in London, who had taken several flights to reach Ladakh, maintained that there was no excuse for me not to go there when I next visited Srinagar.

On my trip to Ladakh I was accompanied by two friends, one of whom drove us there in his own car. We left Srinagar for Zanskar in the morning. I read a feature on

Zanskar in an airline magazine when I was in high school and the images of its stunning landscape have stayed fresh in my mind ever since. I remember stopping midway between Leh and Kargil on my previous trip to Ladakh and found a few bikers transfixed by the barren undulating landscape. One of them compared it to the legendary Mountains of the Moon in Africa.

The first mountain pass on Srinagar Leh highway is the infamous Zoji La. The road is as rough now as it was when I travelled along it 30 years ago. The snow makes it impassable for a good part of the year and the remaining months are spent in clearing the rocks deposited on the road by rainstorms and heavy snowfalls. The road is narrow and steep because it follows a pony track that connected Kashmir with Ladakh before the road was built. There was only one road to cross the Zoji La pass on my maiden journey to Ladakh. Now a new road has been built which is wider but unsurfaced. The friend who drove us, informed me that the new road is used by army trucks with 20 wheels that carry heavy artillery to Kargil. A tunnel is currently being dug under the Zoji La and it will take some years to complete. On the other side of the pass, a bend in the road is called Captain's Turn after an Engineer who fell to his death at the curve during the construction of the road in the 1950s. Some people say that he killed himself because he wanted the entire road to be named after him.

La means 'a mountain pass' in the Tibetan language. My first acquaintance with this two-letter word was the fictional place name, 'Shangri-La', in James Hilton's novel, *Lost Horizon*. Kashmir is described as a 'Shangri-La beneath the summer moon' in an iconic Led Zeppelin song. I recently happened to bump into Robert Plant, the co-writer of the song, in the lift of the hotel where I work and mentioned to him that the lyrics of 'Kashmir' are always buzzing in my head. He told me it was a one-of-a-kind song and couldn't be repeated. In fact, it was Lhasa, on the far side of the Tibetan Plateau, which conjured up the images of a Shangri-La for Kashmiri traders who travelled along the Silk Road. The name *Ladakh* is derived from the Tibetan word, *La-dvags*, which means 'a land of high passes'.

We made a stop at a roadside stall in Drass for a cup of Kashmiri tea in which salt is added instead of sugar. The people in the town have the reputation of making the perfect cup of Kashmiri tea outside The Valley. Drass is a gateway to Ladakh and considered to be one of the coldest inhabited places on the planet during winter. It is lovely in summer. I recall hearing, during my Srinagar childhood, the name of this town in the chanting that characterises the month of Muharram, since the people of Drass and Kargil are mostly Shia Muslims.

We came across a high wall on one side of the road while driving towards the town of Kargil. It was built to hide the convoy of military vehicles from shelling by the Pakistani army positioned on a mountaintop. Some of the shells had landed in Kargil during the war.

We stayed out-of-town in a hotel located on a bank of

the River Suru, an ideal location to explore the Suru Valley. I had heard of the Surma Valley in Bangladesh but not the Suru Valley in my own state. The mountains continually changed colour while we sat on the balcony of the hotel in the evening. It is such a serene place and seems a million miles away from the skirmishes that occasionally take place at what is euphemistically called 'the Line of Control' or LoC. Its name was changed from 'the Ceasefire Line' as a recognition of a de facto border after the two countries went to war for the third time since 1947, the year that India gained independence from Britain. A shopkeeper in Kargil's Lal Chowk suggested that we should go to see a village at the LoC that is less than 10 miles away from the town. He said we could see the other side using binoculars. Although I carried binoculars with me, I didn't think it was a good idea to venture out that far.

The next morning, we left the hotel in Kargil to go to Rangdum. The first section of the road is surfaced and offers resplendent views of the Suru Valley, with green fields enclosed by poplars, willows and apricot trees. I was eager to catch sight of the Nun and Kun peaks on our way to Rangdum, the highest peaks in Kashmir on this side of the LoC. The second highest peak in the world, K2, lies on the other side. It was named by a British surveyor when he sketched two Karakoram peaks from Harmukh, identifying them in his notes by the symbols K1 and K2. I saw the Harmukh peak in my youth and it cast a spell on me that stayed for a long time afterwards. I also remember the famous reply by the 1953 expedition leader, Sir John Hunt, when asked why he wanted to climb Everest: "Because it's there." A very apt answer, I think, perhaps deliberately echoing George Mallory, an earlier climber who is believed to have said it first.

Driving slowly along a fair-weather gravel road from Kargil to Rangdum, we saw many majestic peaks covered in snow but I wasn't sure which ones were Nun and Kun. I mistook two high peaks on the horizon for them until I saw a higher peak shrouded in the clouds behind them. The snow on one of the peaks looked like chiselled marble. I used my binoculars but couldn't ascertain whether it was snow or white stone.

A few miles before reaching Rangdum we passed a camping site with a few tents pitched on the green grass by a mountain stream. As we approached a monastery built on top of a hill in a wide valley, the sunlight at dusk turned the mountains behind the monastery into a palette of beige and brown. When I stood at the monastery I found that the sun had set aflame the trough formed by the slopes of two mountains. It was as beautiful as Turner's painting, *The Fighting Temaraire*. I was awestruck and tried to record the scene on my phone camera but it was too grandly panoramic to be captured by so small a device.

I would have liked to spend the night in a tented enclosure at the foot of the monastery but it was booked by an Italian group expected to arrive that evening so we decided to go to the camping site we had seen on our way to Rangdum.

There is a restaurant and a small hotel at a short distance from the monastery. We stopped at the restaurant for dinner. The hotel restaurant next door was full of French guests. I spoke to a tall Californian in biker gear who was riding his motorbike all the way from Delhi to Ladakh via Manali. He folded his hands in a Namaste gesture before saying that Zanskar is a beautiful place. He had rented a Royal Enfield motorbike in Delhi for 600 rupees a day, which is less than 10 dollars – the price he said that he pays for a sandwich and a cup of coffee in America. He told me that it was the golden age of motorcycling in the Himalayas and was surprised by the number of motorcyclists riding through the Khardung La pass on the way to the Nubra valley. This mountain pass, accessible to motor vehicles of all kinds, is a couple of thousand feet higher than the highest peak in Europe, Mont Blanc.

It was dark by the time we reached the campsite and we used our car headlights to help us search for a spot to pitch our tents. I carried two tents with me but knew how to put up only one of them. The other tent didn't yield and we had to give up and the three of us slept in a tent that had been designed for only two people.

It started to rain at midnight and didn't stop until the early hours of the morning. I thought the campsite must have been greatly affected by the downpour. However, when I unzipped the tent, I found that the ground was dry. The rainwater had seeped into the sandy soil. Once outside our tent we were greeted by a friendly dog. When I spent a night in a tent on my first trekking expedition in Kashmir, I was kept awake the whole night by the barking of a Bakarwal dog who guarded the goats and sheep of the nomads.

There were three or four more tents pitched at the site, belonging to a group of Spanish rock climbers. They had hired a local man to cook for them who sat in a bigger tent that was open on one side. He offered us tea in the morning but wouldn't accept payment for it. I was moved by the genuine hospitality of the Ladakhi people, which made me determined to visit again. I asked one of the Spanish rock climbers if he could show me how to set up my second tent since his tent was somewhat similar to mine. He too found it a complicated task but eventually he succeeded in assembling it.

The people of Kashmir consider Ladakh less appealing than their own valley. However, I was struck by the beauty of the mountainous landscape of shattered rocks in Zanskar. Ladakh has become more attractive for travellers in recent years because it is relatively peaceful. And peace is always beautiful.

*

I had waited all summer in 2010 for the clashes between the security forces and the people to end so I could go to Kashmir for a short stay, but when the protests finally subsided it was the middle of autumn. As Srinagar is a summer capital, it comes to life only from April to September each year. I arrived there in November and the town looked gloomy. I travelled to Gulmarg on a day trip with a few friends but the hill station wore a deserted look. Most of the hotels there had already closed for business until the following summer. We considered ourselves lucky to find a restaurant in a hotel open for lunch. However there were no diners inside. One of my friends asked the solitary waiter there if it was possible to order some food. He said they had only plain rice and a dish of meat that was too dry to be served with rice. I thought it was most courageous of the hotel owners to keep their restaurant open when there were no tourists around.

The situation in Kashmir was relatively peaceful towards the end of 2012. As a consequence, many foreign governments relaxed their advice to their citizens about travelling to Srinagar, and Gulmarg was heralded by the BBC as a new Chamonix. A Polish colleague brought a newspaper from Katowice with him to show me a feature published in its travel pages on Kashmir.

I visited Srinagar again in September 2013 when the then German Ambassador to India, Michael Steiner, hosted a concert by the Bavarian State Orchestra in the Shalimar garden on the outskirts of the city. Zubin Mehta performed at this concert. It created a controversy, resulting in a shutdown of shops and businesses in Srinagar, and so I decided to go to Gulmarg that day.

We drove through a ghost town to reach Gulmarg in a little over an hour. A friend had arranged for us to stay in a cottage owned by the Jammu and Kashmir government. We dropped our bags at the cottage and walked to the far end of Gulmarg, found a newly opened hotel there, and stopped by to have dinner at its restaurant. A receptionist at the hotel told me that they had about 20 rooms out of 80 occupied that night. We were having dinner when I received a phone call from the friend who had arranged the cottage for us, informing us that the caretaker was worried because we hadn't returned yet. It was 10 p.m.

When I returned to Srinagar in August 2016, the authorities had imposed a curfew for a continuous 72 hours. A London acquaintance of mine thought that a curfew in Srinagar meant that no-one was allowed to move around during the night but it was other way round – people in the town could venture out of their homes only in the evening.

When I saw just a handful of Kashmiri people in the aircraft, I wasn't sure if I had boarded the right flight from Delhi to Srinagar. The rest of the passengers were mostly moustachioed men in plain clothes who belonged to the security forces. A lone woman accompanying them had an Indian flag pinned to the lapel of her jacket.

A porter came rushing towards me with a trolley as soon as he saw me standing near the luggage carousel. I usually like to carry my own bags but I couldn't bring myself to say no on this occasion. The main exit of the airport was closed and there was a row of uniformed military men who were perhaps waiting to receive one of their high-ranking officers outside a side door. When one of my relatives drove me to his home near the airport, I heard the crackle of gunfire again after a gap of two decades.

I had no access to the Internet or a phone line, which is ideal if you're on a holiday. But I couldn't call my parents to let them know that I'd reached Srinagar safely. The state government had cut off the Internet and most of the phone lines for more than a month to quell any protests. I tried to make a call using a local sim-card but the message that appeared on my phone screen read 'Congestion'. A few hours later, my relative's neighbour, who subscribed to a government-run mobile service provider and was able to make calls on his phone, appeared with his handset for me to talk to my parents. They had tried in vain to reach the airport to pick me up. It was the small acts of kindness, such as providing me with a handset, that kept people going since the curfew was imposed in mid-July.

Knowing that shops in the town had been shut for many weeks, my friends and acquaintances in London were worried that I might starve in Srinagar if I travelled there. But a thoughtful relative had stocked up on groceries for my visit. Travellers to Kashmir find that hospitality is usually elevated to a high moral principle in the Valley. Perhaps that is why an American head teacher in London suggested to me, when I was looking for a job, that I should work in the hospitality industry. I found that most of the people in Srinagar bore their hardships with dignity and I felt both guilty and touched that my hosts had gone out of their way to arrange everything for my visit.

I borrowed a transistor radio from another neighbour

of theirs to listen to Kashmiri folk music in the evening, since the cable TV channels were scrambled. And I borrowed a book, *The Veiled Suite* by Agha Shahid Ali, from my relative's bookshelf to while away the hours in Kashmir. It had been some time since I'd picked up the collected works of any poet – the last such book I had read was that of Czesław Miłosz. As soon as I started reading Shahid Ali's book I began to relive the years I had spent in Srinagar in the early 1990s. He receives a neat postcard from Kashmir at his home in America and while holding the four-by-six-inch card in his hand he gazes at the half-inch Himalayas. He has a premonition that perhaps this is the closest he can now get to his ancestral home in Srinagar, and the waters of the River Jhelum won't be ultramarine by the time he returns to Kashmir. But he doesn't mind if the idea he has of his birthplace is out of date because he knows that he can develop it into a fine portrait, like developing the negative of a photograph.

The situation in Kashmir reminded me of Borges' favourite theme of circular time, in which things return to where they once were, as many things in Srinagar seem to have come full circle. Telecommunications were disrupted in the early 90s and sometimes people had to travel from Srinagar to Delhi to make an international phone call. I had to phone someone in Delhi to top-up a local sim I was using. However, I could receive calls on it but couldn't dial out. Shahid Ali witnesses the devastation in Kashmir during that time, leading people first to despair and rage, then only rage, then only despair.

'Srinagar hunches like a wild cat,' Shahid writes, 'lonely sentries, wretched in bunkers at the city's bridges, far from their homes in the plains, licensed to kill'. Shahid has been dead for 18 years now and the scene he describes here precedes his death by a dozen years, but it is a true description of the town right now. He quotes the Roman historian, Tacitus, reporting a chieftain's speech which includes the line 'Solitudinum faciunt et pacem appellant' – 'They make a desolation and call it peace'.

While cycling in Srinagar, I passed the high-school I attended and came across a private house at its rear occupied by security forces personnel, one of whom was watching the residents of this neighbourhood from a bunker built on the front lawn. The gates of Badamwari, where almond trees blossomed in the spring, were closed and a plastic tarpaulin hung over them so that no one could have a peek. The nearby temple of Amar Koul was padlocked. It reminded me of a longhaired Englishman who worshipped at this temple from morning till evening during my childhood. The road leading to the top of the Koh-e-Maran hill – once the route of my morning run – was barricaded and an alert paramilitary man armed with a machine gun stood behind a bulletproof van. I walked down the road and saw a signboard pitched by the Jammu and Kashmir Tourism Development Corporation, pointing toward a boat club. I thought that perhaps this desolate road would lead me to a Ghat on Lake Nagin though when I saw the watchtowers of the Central Jail to the right

I felt uneasy. There was a small house at the bottom of the road but I wasn't sure if the area ahead was occupied by paramilitary troops. I certainly didn't want to find myself under arrest for trespassing and end up in hospital.

The mood in Kashmir is one of resignation. However, having gone through the turmoil of the last quarter of a century, the people in the valley have become resilient. I found that socially it is business as usual in Srinagar. I attended the funerals of an elderly relative and a neighbour and received an invitation to attend a wedding. Businessmen have become oblivious of their losses and those who are hard up are suffering in silence. The groups of young men lurking in the back roads of Srinagar could easily get into trouble by throwing stones at the security forces to overcome their boredom. But it is very difficult for someone born and brought up in Kashmir not to be troubled by the troubles in the Valley, no matter if that person is living in a faraway country. Shahid describes his émigré life as if he were an Adam of two Edens, a man who has lost paradise twice, and he has a nightmarish vision of being rowed through paradise on a river of hell.

I could get around in Srinagar on my pushbike. Rumour had it in the town that petrol supplies had been stopped. The petrol stations indeed remained shut and I saw children selling the tawny liquid in small water bottles by the roadside. I left my parents' home early one morning to cycle to the home of a friend who lives on the slope of a mountain at the edge of Lake Dal, and he showed me a stream that I'd heard of but never seen before. We took a walk along it to reach the Shalimar Garden, accompanied by a chorus of cicadas. It offered me a panoramic view of the valley with Lake Dal in the foreground and the Koh-e-Maran hill in the middle. The fort built on top of this hill in 1808 was opened to the public again recently after more than twenty years, and many people said that Srinagar was going to be the next big tourist destination in Asia.

The peace is always fragile in Kashmir. Before I booked my tickets in advance, I'd asked a friend if August was the right time to visit Srinagar. He said it was never the right time to visit the Valley and I could only hope for a peaceful visit. I would have liked to stay in a guesthouse called Dar-es-Salam (which means House of Peace) overlooking Lake Nagin but I stayed at my parents' home and, while there, Agha Shahid Ali's 'The Veiled Suite' transported me to a House of Sorrow. The poet accompanies the coffin of his mother, who has died of brain cancer, in a Lufthansa flight from America for a burial in his ancestral graveyard in Kashmir. Shahid's grief for his dead mother turns into grief for his lost homeland in the elegies he writes on this journey. He has imagined that he is the only passenger on a flight from Delhi to Srinagar. When I flew from London to New Delhi to catch a connecting flight to Srinagar I was awoken from a similar dream.

London Regained

For a long time, the description of London as 'the great mean city' by Irish poet Louis MacNeice, rang true because I was living a lonely life in this big metropolis. I often listened to Diana Krall's melancholy rendering of the song, *Boulevard of Broken Dreams*, and found a kind of solace in the line, 'The joy you find here you borrow'. However, I knew there were a lot of people besides me who lived that way. As for the Londoners of my acquaintance who were fortunate enough to enjoy regular companionship, most seemed to have met their partners elsewhere.

I had got to know someone in the West End who was an artist in chatting up women and I was astonished by his craftsman-like technique. When I commented on it one day, he said it wasn't that difficult to find a partner in London if you can take a woman out for a meal and entertain her. In those days, however, I found it difficult to feed myself properly, let alone pay for someone else's meal.

For me, the only real connection with London for the first 7 years was the daily grind. After working in a corner shop for a year and a half, I was surprised to be granted a week's holiday, but I asked to return to work after only three days. A neighbour in Hampstead was flabbergasted to learn that I wasn't offered the full statutory annual leave at work. It hadn't bothered me because I didn't know what to do with my days off and it cost money to socialise in London.

There came a time when I couldn't care less about being on my own but enjoyed my solitary pursuits, such as sitting in a coffee shop and reading a book in the evening after finishing my work for the day. And just when I had finally given up the idea of finding someone in London, my sister arranged for me to meet a woman from our neighbourhood in Srinagar. I married her a month later in a hotel in Gurgaon.

It was in 2012 – the year when London was to host the summer Olympic Games. I eagerly waited for several months for my wife to join me in London but the British High Commission in Delhi delayed issuing her visa for so long that I was on the brink of leaving London and moving back to Kashmir for good. After much wrangling with the Home Office, someone at the High Commission in New Delhi contacted me by email to tell me to send my wife to the embassy to collect her Spouse Visa.

The town was looking festive as I took my wife, who had never visited London before, on a sightseeing tour of the city the day after she arrived. A cable car to cross the Thames had just opened and I took her on board to show her the Olympic Village from above. After living in London for 18 years, I had become a jolly tourist. It wasn't for long, though, because my wife found out that she was going to have a baby.

Fatherhood revealed the kinder aspect of London as I started riding buses with a pushchair. A stranger would offer me a hand when I was trying to climb up a flight of steps at an Underground station with a buggy. It was as if by magic, so it seemed to me, that an invisible resident had become apparent and was at long last noticed by his fellow residents. It was around this time that I came across Cyril Connolly's pronouncement that, for a writer, 'the pram in the hallway' is one of the 'enemies of promise.' And I remembered that in one of VS Naipaul's books, when someone asked him during his travels if he had any children, his reply was that if he had he wouldn't have written any books. Many years later I heard Naipaul fondly refer to his wife Nadira's daughter from a previous marriage as 'daughter of my wife'. To me, that certainly sounded better than 'stepdaughter'. It was in 2016, three years after the birth of my son, that I at last found the inspiration to work on a book again. However, I realize that there are plenty of women writers who produce books after having given birth, and therefore a male writer ought not to say that becoming a parent will inhibit his creative life.

I began to see my adopted hometown anew through the eyes of my son. Like him I experienced wonder when I saw daisies, dandelions and buttercups sprouting in the grass in springtime. Nursery rhymes that I had never heard before sounded as if they belonged to me. Once, on a trip to a local library with my son, a librarian commented that the future of the textile industry in the country looked great after he'd led a group of children in singing and miming 'Wind the Bobbin Up'.

With my son in a stroller, I frequented parks and gardens again. I had passed an arboretum near my home for many years but never walked through it until it became a playground for my little boy for a year or two. I also took him to my favourite patch of the Heath during the summer. However, life became easier for me when I got a child seat for my bike. I had thought it would be cumbersome to ride my bike to work with a child seat attached to it, not realizing that you could detach it from the bike at the push of a button. The school 'run' became 'a walk in the park' after I started cycling my son to school on my bike. In our neighbourhood, there was only one other parent – a Dutchman – carrying his child to school on a bike. Cruising downhill on my bike with my son to reach his school is a joy, and sometimes his classmates who are walking to school, shout his name when they see us whiz past them.

The school arranges a breakfast once a year for cyclist parents but I skip it in case I turn out to be the only one there. A neighbour has suggested that I should get a tandem bike to cycle my son to school but I think it is time for him to ride his own bike.

I cycle in London throughout the year, come rain or come shine. In fact, London has an unfair reputation for bad weather. Perhaps it is because Londoners are used to starting their small talk with that topic. When I talk to my mother on the phone and ask her about the weather in Srinagar, she usually feels offended that I would talk to her about something as trivial as that during a long-distance call. I remember seeing an art-house Bollywood film on television as a child in which a man tells a woman he is dating, in order to break her silence, that English people like to talk about the weather when they meet for the first time. For my part, when I tried to engage in conversation with people in the Hampstead corner shop, I learned to use such useful words as 'nippy' and 'mild'.

Because the rain that falls in London is usually light, you tend not to get caught in torrential downpours very often. Sometimes it doesn't rain for weeks on end, and yet visitors to London expect it to rain every day. An acquaintance in Kashmir once mentioned to me that he owned "a long raincoat made by London Fog". However, I'd not seen any fog or mist in London, nor heard of any clothing company called 'London Fog'. A friend from Kashmir who was a fan of Sherlock Holmes was surprised to find when he visited London that no one wears deerstalker hats anymore.

A taxi driver who once drove me along the Holloway Road stated, amongst a litany of complaints, that London was a polluted, crime-ridden city. In fact, the sky over London looks pristine if you come from New Delhi. An irate air-hostess who wasn't happy with a laundry service in London once confided to me that her clothes smelt as if they'd been washed in the polluted water of Mumbai, only to pause momentarily, realizing I might come from there, and then apologized for her outburst. I overheard an American businessman, who had travelled from Mumbai to London, saying that he was shocked to see the Mumbai streets so rubbish-strewn. He had thought that Delhi was appalling until he travelled to Mumbai.

I have never felt the need for a fan during summers in London. The heat isn't usually stifling, and winters are milder than in many Central European countries. When a lady visiting London from Delhi expressed her wish to breathe fresh air during the night, I suggested that she keep her bedroom window open. She was startled and asked, "What about the mosquitoes?" This lady had chosen to live on the top floor of a high-rise building in Delhi, high enough that mosquitoes couldn't reach there to bite her whenever she opened the window of her flat. I assured her that she wouldn't find that a problem in London (though certain types of mosquito do exist here).

It took me many years to understand the yearning of Robert Browning in the lines 'Oh to be in England / Now that April's there'. My Punjabi landlord warned me about showers in April when I moved into a room in his house in Hampstead. Later I heard someone citing the proverb that April showers bring May flowers. It was indeed pleasing to see rose gardens in London blossom in the month of May. If someone wants to escape the heat in Punjab in April, they will certainly long for the kind of showers we have in London. I often encounter hotel guests from heat-stricken countries who feel dismayed if it doesn't rain during their stay. I once came across some children from just such a parched country collecting snow in carrier bags from the forecourt of the hotel to take up to their room and play with like sand, only to be most disappointed to find it had melted by the time they got back to their room.

I like autumn in London more than spring, which is heralded by the blossoming of Japanese cherry trees. But it is when I walk through an alley in my neighbourhood in autumn that I feel elation on seeing the crimson leaves of a Japanese maple. The big trees lining the walking path at the south side of the Heath shed their leaves in autumn and I see the habitual walkers wading through them in their wellington boots. Some of them carry cameras slung over their shoulders in readiness to take pictures when the autumn light is good. Hampstead residents eagerly don summer clothes in the spring just as they tend to wear or carry hats and coats in the autumn, no doubt because of the often swiftly changing weather. I once saw a local resident sitting in a coffee shop in winter, wearing only a vest on top and even then he was perspiring.

It snowed a few centimetres just one day after I moved to Hampstead and I saw a lot of people gathered at the top of Parliament Hill. The children were dragging plastic toboggans with ropes. It was a most picturesque scene. But the city seems ill-prepared for snow, which causes chaos on the roads. I had seen the grit boxes all over the city during my first few months here and wondered what they were for. The depots actually ran out of gritting salt when it turned unusually cold one winter.

At first I found it amusing to hear Londoners talk about the hot weather whenever the temperature reached the mid-20s. The corner shop in Hampstead ran out of ice cream when the mercury touched 30 degrees. During the summer, Hampstead Heath becomes a picnic ground and crowds of people carrying blankets and baskets can be seen walking towards it on the weekends. Some of the men sport Panama hats and linen shorts and some of the women wear sarongs. However, the locals of Hampstead mostly go abroad during the summer months, in the footsteps of Byron, Shelley and Keats, and they still prefer to call the other side of the English Channel 'the Continent'.

*

London not only serves as a film location but is also a genre in itself. I had read the book, *84 Charing Cross Road*, by Helene Hanff, and some time later watched the film version in which the American bibliophile is played by Anne Bancroft and the obliging bookseller by Anthony Hopkins. I had searched for the number '84' on Charing Cross Road only to find the premises empty. Today there is a McDonald's at this site. There were still a number of second-hand bookshops in Charing Cross when I worked around there. Some of those shops are now selling herbal medicine and other such products. In those days there was also a shop in Charing Cross Road that sold film posters and picture postcards of such scary British actors as Boris Karloff.

I had witnessed London landmarks in a Bollywood film

when I was a student in Srinagar. It was thrilling to see Tower Bridge projected on a big screen and a glamorous film star playing cat and mouse with a villain on the Thames. However, after having lived in London for a few years, I realized that showing Bollywood actors and actresses breaking into song in Hyde Park or the Underground on the spur of the moment actually takes some pre-planning – though not as much as is required for home-grown London location shooting. Getting permission for an entire street to be closed off can cost a British company a hefty sum; whereas a small Bollywood film crew, with far fewer technical personnel involved in what is a comparatively shoe-string operation, simply drives around town in a van, picks a location on the spot, jumps out and shoots.

There were two or three cinemas in Srinagar that showed American and British films in the mornings, their titles translated into Urdu on the billboards. These titles, borrowed from Bollywood films, were outlandish. A title like *Billion Dollar Brain* would be translated into something like *Killer Instinct* in Urdu. On one occasion, a local cinema showed a Tamil film with a title irrelevantly translated as For One Night Only, evidently to give the impression that the film belonged to the 'adult' genre.

Most of the people who thronged to these morning showings didn't understand the films with English dialogue but that didn't matter as they were generally there to enjoy scenes of a sexual nature, Western style. But I was more dazzled to see the cityscapes of New York and San Francisco in an American film than a scantily clad woman marooned on a tropical island.

Sometimes, in the West End of London, I watched a film for as little as £2 in a repertory cinema. At other times I would notice a crowd gathered outside the Odeon cinema in Leicester Square for the premiere of some Hollywood blockbuster. I finally got a chance to go inside this cinema in 2012 when I accompanied the documentary film-maker, Marc Isaacs, to the opening of the London Film Festival, having been featured in a small role in *The Road*, one of his London-based documentaries. The cinema was far bigger than I'd imagined, reminding me of a visit I made with friends to a cinema in Jaipur in which the hall looked positively palatial. Not for nothing were the great cinema houses of the 1930s called 'picture palaces'.

Bollywood had a love affair with Kashmir and shot many of the musical sequences for its films in the Valley. The word would go out in Srinagar that a film crew was going to shoot at a certain location on a particular day, and children and adults alike would flock to the site. On one cold winter day, I saw a female Bollywood extra on a pair of skis, wearing a short dress and propped up by two men on a ski slope. There were goose pimples on her legs and she shivered in the cold, whereas the men who held her upright wore woollen balaclavas to keep themselves warm. How sad, I thought, that she had to endure such discomfort in order to make a living by entertaining the filmgoers of India.

On a summer's day, I saw a houseboat moored to the bank of the River Jhelum being used for the shooting of an English language film. It was a quiet scene and, surprisingly, there was no crowd of gaping onlookers. Someone told me later that the location was used in the filming of David Lean's *A Passage to India*. One of the cottages and some viewing points in Kashmir were named after the Bollywood films in which these locations featured. An entire mountain valley has even been named after a Bollywood film since it was used as a location for the filming of a romantic musical sequence.

It was only after a television serial was shot at Lake Dal that people living on the shore in Srinagar became aware of what the sons of the houseboat owners were up to. This serial became an instant hit all over India; but film location tourists were already shunning Srinagar in 1991, as it had become a risky destination. Rather than spotting a glamorous Bollywood star driving in a jeep along a road flanked by tall poplars, you would find only TV crews reporting from a trouble-spot. It marked the end of an era for Indian cinema.

*

After I moved to Hampstead, I happened to read a poem by John Hands about Waterlow Park in Highgate. He describes how lonely people living in the neighbourhood trickle out after a rainfall for a walk in the park. One day I took a walk across the Heath to reach Waterlow Park and, although I found it scenically appealing, its description by the poet kept ringing in my head. I thought it was great to have accessible gardens and parks, offering solace to lonely Londoners. Later, I learnt that Waterlow Park was given to the public by its owner so that it could become a 'garden for the garden-less'.

I was confounded in the beginning to see how many people came to Hampstead Heath to walk their dogs. Sometimes I saw a dog-walker with half a dozen different breeds trailing behind her. The corner shop in Hampstead where I worked stocked greeting cards with pictures of cats printed on them and those cards sold very well. The lady who supplied them (an American Hampstead-dweller) told me that people living in Hampstead loved cats and dogs, which is why she had decided to make greeting cards depicting cats, the pet that she herself preferred.

I found the sight of small parks in Central London more enchanting than the big Royal Parks and Gardens when I roamed the streets on my bicycle. Sometimes I would turn a corner and come across a green enclosure where office workers were eating sandwiches during their lunch hour. And, just as many Italian towns are built around a central piazza, London seemed to have been built around squares that are actually parks.

The home county of Kent might be called the Garden of England but it is the gardens of London, which one sometimes glimpses while travelling by bus or bike, that are truly captivating. In fact it was the flowers grown in baskets hung outside pubs that I found particularly charming. The exterior of one fish and chip shop in the West End was likewise adorned with flowerpots. I usually saw its owner – an old man from Cyprus – using a hooked metal pipe attached to a rubber hose to water his potted plants. It is always a pleasure to see a gardener at work. During my first few months in London I often saw, on my way to the library, a uniformed gardener tending flowerbeds at the roadside.

I found the displays of flowers outside florists in different London neighbourhoods at once attractive and intriguing. An aproned florist picking flowers one by one from each bucket under the awnings was a joy to behold. However, I was puzzled that people in London bought flowers for their loved ones. When I told an acquaintance in Kashmir that Londoners like to take a bouquet of fresh flowers when they visit a relative or friend, he was even more puzzled than I was that you could give something like flowers, which don't last long, as a gift.

Some of these London florists have set up their stalls in forlorn places. On my way to work I pass a florist under a marquee pitched at the edge of the Heath – the only shop in the vicinity – and there is another near a water fountain with a conical roof at the bottom of Fitzjohn's Avenue. On Valentine's Day, they are still open at night, selling roses to motorists who have perhaps forgotten to buy them for their spouses during the day. There is even a florist further along Park Road that is open 24 hours – a rarity in London where most shops close at 6 pm.

In Kashmir, wedding hosts sometimes invite gardeners working in a public garden to bring some fresh flowers to a wedding in exchange for joining the wedding feast. The petals of these free flowers are thrown like confetti. It is customary to throw sweets and coins at a bride or groom, to be retrieved by children who fight hard to pick up such valuables from the floor. I recall it being like a rugby scrum, too rough for me, which is why, as a child, I preferred to be a spectator rather than a player at Srinagar weddings. On a trip to Kashmir a year ago, I was surprised to find that a shop had opened in a touristy part of Srinagar selling artificial flowers and it was busy with people buying plastic flowers to decorate their cars for weddings. The flowers looked so real from a distance that I mistook the shop assistant for a genuine florist selling fresh flowers.

I'd lived in London for all of seven years before I started working in a hotel and thus became fully aware of the fact that a florist plays an important role in decorating a venue for a London wedding. One day, a florist handed me a few bunches of flowers for a wedding at the hotel, explaining that the bunches had to weigh a little more and be full of flowers in order to look as good as they should in the hands of the bridesmaids. Another florist left a few single white roses to be worn on the lapels of the tuxedos worn by the friends of the groom. However, the decorative white flowers customarily displayed for a wake are sometimes deliberately left behind by bereaved family members.

I wasn't accustomed to seeing fresh flowers in Kashmir out of season and was therefore surprised to find red roses being sold throughout the year in London. While walking in the West End late at night I often saw a theatrical-looking man in a dark suit and brilliant white shoes carrying a bucket full of roses and offering each of them for sale to any couple he saw holding hands. When I saw him for the first time, I thought he had wandered out of the set of the neighbouring production of *The Phantom of the Opera*. In the daytime, I would see an Irishwoman who claimed to be a clairvoyant handing out some small sprigs held together by a piece of kitchen foil and asking for money in exchange. An elderly friend who remembers often witnessing the same "Lucky Heather" appeal in the West End during the 1950s expressed surprise when I told him that it was still going strong in the 1990s.

*

I got into the habit of drinking coffee in Marin County, California, before coming to London. I frequented a coffee shop in downtown Mill Valley that had a stack of sacks containing coffee beans inside the shop, making for a highly aromatic ambiance. It was an atmospheric place where cyclists would drop in to grab a coffee. Although I travelled to other cities in America, the distinctive taste of Californian coffee lingered in my mouth.

I became a coffee shop habitué once again when I arrived in London and discovered a coffee shop in Covent

Garden. The price of a cup in those days was less than a pound, and you could sit there with an open book and empty cup for as long as you wanted. A year later, I saw a crowd one night outside a small coffee shop in Frith Street and was able to walk inside only with difficulty. The coffee they served there tasted superior, and when I saw the name of the shop on a poster on the wall, I realised it was the renowned Bar Italia, about which I had often read or heard favourable reports. I subsequently stopped by from time to time and it was there that I tasted a custard tart for the first time. Someone told me many years later that this delicious cinnamon-dusted tart was called 'pastel de nata' and originated in Portugal. I also came across a restaurant called 'The Coffee Cup' in Hampstead that was often mentioned in the local papers. But I never had the courage to order just a cup of coffee there, even though I walked by it many times.

I got to know other neighbourhoods in London mostly by their coffee shops, where I would make a stop while cycling through. A friend, who often saw me in one such coffee shop in Camden, liked to jokingly call the shop by my name. There weren't many great coffee shops in London 25 years ago but nowadays you can find quite a variety of them, including one where you can also get your bicycle fixed and one for cat lovers in which you can have a coffee and stroke a cat at the same time.

When I lived in Mill Valley for a few months I had become familiar with the German compound noun *kaffeeklatsch* in its English usage – an informal social gathering for coffee and conversation. However, the customs of Californian café society did not reach London until a decade later. A few coffee shops in London were run by the Seattle Coffee Company. One day I found that one of its branches had turned into Starbucks and soon this American chain became ubiquitous in London. It occurred to me that Londoners thronged there not so much for the taste of their coffee but to stretch their legs while eating a sandwich. The price of a hot meal in a restaurant in London is many times more than the price of a sandwich in a café. I once mentioned to an editor of a West End neighbourhood magazine that there weren't a lot of restaurants in Central London that served healthy food and she looked at me askew. Perhaps I ought to have added the word 'affordable' to my claim.

If familiarity breeds contempt, it certainly applies to the town where one lives. I recently commented to some Venetian guests staying at the hotel that their hometown is pretty and they replied that they found London prettier. I have travelled as far as Andalusia just to see a UNESCO World Heritage Site but never been inside the one on my doorstep – the Tower of London. Perhaps that's because of my reluctance to see the Kohinoor diamond, which was acquired by the British as part of the spoils of war, along with Kashmir and Hazara, after the fall of the Sikh Empire. Kashmir – and its people – were sold by the East India Company for a paltry sum, thereby sowing the seeds of a conflict which is still raging in the region today.

Admittedly, I have sometimes felt tempted to enter the Tower when showing its exterior to friends visiting London but I have yet to succumb. However, as a cycling enthusiast whose father rode a Raleigh bike, I could not fail to be aware that Sir Walter Raleigh was imprisoned in the Tower. I have read an account of Raleigh's doomed expedition to El Dorado in Naipaul's *A Way in the World*.

When I read the poem, *Vacillation*, by WB Yeats, I stumbled upon a mystic tree which is 'half all glittering flame and half all green' and 'half and half consume what they renew'. I felt that this symbolised London, where old structures disappear and new ones rise in a never-ending cycle. It occurred to me that I shouldn't seek new landscapes but cultivate a fresh outlook in order to apprehend a Proustian universe in which to sit with an open book and empty cup in a coffee shop is time regained.

November 2018 – October 2019

ACKNOWLEDGEMENTS

My sincere gratitude to Asia, Adam, Arne and all of my friends and acquaintances who have made this book possible. I am also indebted to my editors, Robert Lambolle and Maya Hornick, for their invaluable input and support.

Sorrows of the Moon

A Journey Through London

'Iqbal Ahmad loves people, cities, details, history and poetry with a true clear writerly attention. The structures and appalling current dilemma of his own birthplace were created by the empire run from this city - this London seen by the sad, learned, compassionate eyes of a man from Srinagar. Read it and weep: and be grateful for its subtlety, courtesy and depth.'

RUTH PADEL

'Like Baudelaire's sorrowful moon he "drops a furtive tear" for his homeland; but perhaps we are left with a sliver of hope in the image of Ahmed's old moon and his new united in a single vision.'

SAMEER RAHIM in *TLS*

'Iqbal Ahmed's *Sorrows of the Moon* appears, at first, to be wide-eyed and innocent. It soon reveals itself as a Mayhew excursion through the cruel and fantastic city we are forced to recognize as our own.'

IAIN SINCLAIR in *The Guardian*

BY THE SAME AUTHOR

Empire of the Mind

A Journey Through Great Britain

'Iqbal Ahmed's *Empire of the Mind* is an elegant epistle of disillusion. Though he arrives in Britain hoping to find what his US guidebook describes as the "genuinely most civilised" country, Iqbal discovers it has "one of the world's largest prison populations". Feeling similarly circumscribed, he brilliantly observes the chilly, rootless life lived by many immigrants. A snack on Bournemouth Pier sums up the seedy blandness of the former hub of empire: "The chips were tasty but the fish didn't seem so fresh. Evidently that didn't matter." '

CHRISTOPHER HIRST in *The Independent*

'Fascinating, humorous and poignant'

LAURIE HARDIMAN in *The Times*

'A great tenderness of spirit suffuses this book.'

MURROUGH O'BRIEN in *The Independent on Sunday*

Beatrice's Last Smile

A Journey Through Germany

'A profound comment on identity and belonging in today's troubled multicultural world'

MUNEEZA SHAMSIE in *Dawn*

'Reveals a reality that cannot be captured by mainstream reportage.'

LILIAN PIZZICHINI

'A finely written account of hidden lives. Vital reading.'

SAMEER RAHIM, Arts and Books Editor, *Prospect*

'A voyage of discovery away from a lost paradise'

DAPHNE CHAMBERLAIN in *The Archer*

'A wonderful book by a brilliant and unusual writer.'

VANORA BENNETT

Iqbal Ahmed was born in Kashmir in 1968 and has lived in London since 1994. His previous books have been chosen as Books of the Year: *Sorrows of the Moon* in The Guardian and The Independent on Sunday, and *Empire of the Mind* in The Economist.